The Rise
of the **Platform**
Marketer

The Rise of the Platform Marketer

Performance Marketing with Google, Facebook, and Twitter, Plus the Latest High-Growth Digital Advertising Platforms

Craig Dempster

John Lee

WILEY

Printed in the United States of America.

10 9 8 7 6 5 4 3 2 1

Contents

Foreword

In 25 years leading a growing, evolving customer relationship marketing company, I have witnessed a number of major industry shifts, propelled by advancements in technology, increased access to data, and improvements in analytic techniques. The digitization of just about everything in the lives of consumers has brought about the greatest shift of all—the ability for marketers to customize the brand experience to the individual customer. Through personalized interactions that take place via online and offline media and channels, across multiple screens and platforms, throughout the customer lifecycle, today's marketer can truly optimize the value of the customer portfolio. The opportunity of addressability at scale far surpasses those of eras past.

My colleagues, Craig Dempster and John Lee, were among the forward-thinking leaders who recognized this opportunity early on. Together, we spent the first few years of this decade developing a customer relationship marketing (CRM) approach we call Connected CRM (cCRM)®, which has proven itself in activating customer-centric strategies for Merkle's Fortune 1000 clients.

My 2014 book, *Connected CRM: Implementing a Data-Driven, Customer-Centric Business Strategy,* outlined a highly structured organizational framework for building customer strategy as a business strategy. The concept of the Platform Marketer was first introduced in that book as the persona that harnesses a new set of skills necessary to operate within the cCRM framework. And in the year since it was written, Craig and John have been closely involved with clients who are establishing and executing cCRM strategies.

With that experience, we have expanded our thinking. We have cultivated a deeper understanding of the addressable audience platforms and further honed the Platform Marketer skills, whose influence and complexity we didn't fully realize when I wrote *cCRM*.

As the market's movement toward digital accelerates, so does the movement of marketing spend, with brands investing in new technologies that enable addressability in all their customer interactions. These growing and constantly fragmenting digital audience platforms, such as Facebook, Google, and Twitter, are the new frontier of marketing. They open countless avenues for creating relevant engagements with consumers. The opportunity is so vast and multifaceted, we've come to realize that marketers must begin to retool themselves, at the most foundational level, in order to master the rapidly proliferating digital platform opportunity.

In writing *The Rise of the Platform Marketer,* the authors enlisted the support of a team of expert contributors, authorities in their own fields of study, to ensure that the content is comprehensive, accurate, and adaptable not only across industries but over time and through constant change. They have expertly outlined the competencies required to remain relevant in marketing today, producing results that include not only competitive advantage for your organization, but for the individual reader—*the Platform Marketer*. I hope marketers will read this book and absorb the valuable skills needed to stay up to speed on the digital audience platforms and capitalize on the opportunity of addressability at scale.

David Williams
Chairman and CEO, Merkle

Preface

For decades, the concept of customer relationship marketing (CRM) has attracted executives who believe in customer centricity and the idea that customer strategy should be the basis of the business strategy. In his book, *Connected CRM: Implementing a Data-Driven, Customer-Centric Business Strategy*, David Williams defines Connected CRM (cCRM)® as the systematic practice in which marketers identify, acquire, and retain customers based upon their value. Through a framework that supports these orchestrated customer interactions, brands are able to improve financial results, create competitive advantage, and drive shareholder value.[1]

As marketers, we've always known that the key to competitive advantage is to be the brand that better understands the needs and behaviors of individual consumers. That intelligence allows the brand to create greater value through more personalized, relevant experiences. Over the years,

---

[1] David Williams, *Connected CRM: Building a Data-Driven, Customer-Centric Business Strategy* (Hoboken, NJ: John Wiley & Sons, March 2014).

advancements in data management, technology, and analytics have continuously enhanced our capacity to build vital customer intelligence.

More recently, the mass digitization of media and channels has allowed marketers to take that knowledge to another level, driving ever more personalized engagements with individual consumers, delivered across the complete range of media, channels, and devices. Today, the market refers to just about everything as media. As a marketer, you have countless avenues for addressing consumers, whether by reaching the audience through third-party sources, such as display or search (paid); building buzz through social communities, industry chatter, or even public relations (earned); or by making first-party connections via your own properties, such as website or mobile apps (owned).

Addressability at scale is the opportunity to create competitive advantage through the delivery of targeted, personalized experiences to consumers. Media and channels that are enabled by addressability at scale can be described as "addressable audience platforms." An audience platform is a digital technology that enables those automated experiences to individuals (known and anonymous), at scale, utilizing first- and/or third-party data. Every interaction is an opportunity to collect and leverage data. But only now it has become possible to manage these disparate interactions at scale, as the digital audience platforms, such as Facebook, Google, and Twitter, continue to develop and grow. And our ability to build such wide-reaching connections across the addressable platforms has enabled us to foster relationships that span the customer life cycle and thus optimize the value of customers and segments.

To develop such relevant engagements with consumers through these platforms, brands are beginning to realize that they will have to cultivate an elevated set of capabilities, tools, metrics, and processes, along with a new set of skills to utilize them. This new breed of marketer—the Platform Marketer—has a deep understanding of traditional marketing and CRM principals, yet possesses the knowledge and innovative forethought to thrive in the ever-expanding digital audience platform environment. Due to the increased complexity involved in leveraging data, technology, and analytics in the digital era, platform marketing is not for the faint of heart or the complacent. Successful Platform Marketers will be steadfast innovators, dedicated to navigating undiscovered territory, wrought with twists, turns, and heavy lifting. But for those who can capitalize on addressability at scale, the spoils will include more profitable customer relationships and sustained competitive advantage.

Acknowledgments

Even before David Williams's book, *Connected CRM*, hit the virtual display shelves of Amazon, we already had our sights set on a follow-up book. We knew that marketers would require a whole new set of competencies in order to execute on a Connected CRM (cCRM) strategy and take advantage of the opportunity of addressability at scale that is made possible by the digital audience platforms. So we rounded up our colleagues who are widely recognized as leading experts in the capricious fields of data, analytics, technology, and organizational consulting. In the ensuing months, we worked together to construct what we believe will be the preeminent guide for marketers who are ready to achieve customer centricity in the age of digital.

There is one reason we felt the sense of freedom, the confidence, and the latitude to follow through with our vision for this book: the leadership of David Williams. He has shaped Merkle into a platform upon which his team can learn, grow, err, and succeed through experiences that help not only our clients to flourish, but also our company and our own careers.

He has nurtured a culture that breeds innovation, bringing together some of the smartest minds in the marketing world to tackle the tough challenges of a constantly shifting marketing landscape.

We owe a very special thanks to all of the subject matter experts and their teams who contributed to the chapters: Patrick Collins, Peter Kemp, Matthew Mobley, Matthew Naeger, Megan Pagliuca, Bennie Smith, Leah van Zelm, Peter Vandre, Anudit Vikram, Kevin Walsh, and Zimm Zimmermann. Without their expertise in the critical building blocks of the Platform Marketer competencies, we couldn't have written this book at the level of detail required to materially impact the reader ready to hone these skills.

We would also like to acknowledge the vital role played by Sherri Aycoth, who is the heart and soul of our communications, with her unique aptitude for capturing our team's ideas and vision and bringing them to life in words. Over the years, she has shown undying commitment, playing a key writing role in both *Connected CRM* and *The Rise of the Platform Marketer*, in addition to her lead marketing communications role for Merkle. We could not have completed this book without her steadfast dedication to company, team, and mission.

And for her fearless leadership of Merkle's marketing organization, we thank Jeaneen Andrews-Feldman, SVP and chief orchestrator of the many levers it took to keep this project on path. Her invaluable relationships with the executive committee, the content team, the marketing and PR teams, the publisher, the media, and our clients have made months of effort move smoothly forward to fruition.

Finally, our most important recognition goes out to our families for their ongoing support, not just during the writing of this book, but throughout our careers. There is no way we could succeed in this business without spending time outside our day jobs, partnering together and reflecting on the future of marketing. The time we spend on the road is time not spent with family, and we owe them a debt of gratitude for their patience and encouragement—and for always being there to back us up on the home front. It's only through that support that we feel free to pursue new ideas and innovations that elevate the potential for marketing success.

—Craig & John

Chapter 1 The Age of the Customer

Customer relationship marketing (CRM) isn't merely about the implementation of a tactical marketing plan. A true customer-centric business strategy requires a fundamental shift in the organization's framework—its leadership, its priorities, its processes, even its culture. These changes result in a new paradigm for the company's goals, its customers' expectations, and its trajectory for the future. The force behind this shift is the state of today's consumer marketplace, which can be characterized as the *age of the customer*.

Think back to the brand revolution of the 1950s, when the advent of national television broadcasting created coast-to-coast demand and brand recognition. The companies that had the vision and resources to seize the opportunity and take their brands nationwide were the clear winners. Brands like Tide and Chevrolet became household names across the country, triumphing over smaller companies that faded away in their wake during the *age of the brand*.

The channel revolution was symbolic of the 1990s and early 2000s. It exploded when online marketers like Amazon and eBay changed the meaning of "going shopping" by making Internet purchasing commonplace. And GEICO, a proven insurance industry innovator, managed to shift the buying norm by introducing consumers to a whole new way to shop for insurance. Today, 13.1 percent of Americans are considered digital natives,[1] having never known a time when the world was not at their fingertips. The result of this way of life is an unfathomable amount of data that can either overwhelm marketers or help them increase their customer knowledge and drive strong relationships.

During the *age of the channel*, marketers like Capital One and GEICO pioneered the use of individual-level data and analytics to target and personalize direct marketing efforts that drove new customer acquisition and strengthened customer relationships. The innovative application of analytics on valuable first-party data (owned customer information) and third-party data (acquired from data providers) within direct mail and telemarketing (the addressable media of the day) resulted in massive scale and efficiencies. These one-to-one trailblazers recognized the market opportunity of the moment, and like Tide and Chevrolet before them, they capitalized on it. They used a strategy of addressability at scale to gain enormous market share in highly competitive markets.

Today, we're facing another moment-in-time opportunity to harness the power of addressability at scale. Simply defined, this refers to the application of data and analytics to drive highly efficient, individual-level targeting and personalized experiences to consumers—and doing it at massive scale. It is now the *age of the customer*, where consumers are empowered with the tools to make their own purchase decisions— and they know how to use them. The gateway to competitive dominance lies in the addressable audience platforms that are being created for the "always-on consumer," who engages with brands through digital media and channels, across multiple screens and platforms, 24/7. Leading third-party providers are scaling their platforms to deliver the experiences consumers seek, while creating an addressable marketing stage for advertisers. Some of these are household names, such as AOL, Facebook, and Twitter, providing tools for advertisers to

---

[1] www.nbcnews.com/id/53255563/ns/technology_and_science-science/t/digital-natives-most-least-wired-countries-revealed/#.VQimiGR4pEE.

reach their logged-in users. Others, like Rubicon Project and App-Nexus, are little known technology players that are leveraging their place in the ad delivery ecosystem to create addressable experiences across an open web of thousands of publishers. The competition for advertising dollars among the major platform players is driving increased targeting, tracking, and content capabilities that continually enhance the opportunity for the marketer to implement addressable consumer experiences.

The opportunity for efficiency and scale within the addressable audience platforms dwarfs that of the aforementioned offline direct marketing opportunity of the channel age. In our opinion, it is poised to generate many times the value for those companies willing to take first-mover advantage. Further, due to the increased complexity of leveraging data and analytics in today's digital world, addressability at scale will create more enduring competitive power for those leaders.

CREATING COMPETITIVE ADVANTAGE THROUGH THE DIGITAL AUDIENCE PLATFORMS

The opportunity for brands to create competitive advantage rests squarely on their ability to achieve addressability at scale. Addressability at scale is enabled through the application of data and analytics to the digital audience platform marketplace that is now at massive scale. And CRM is all about using addressability to increase the targetability, relevance, and measurement of marketing impressions and experiences across the customer lifecycle, in all channels and media, both online and offline.

Consumers are changing every day in the ways they interact with brands—shifting their media consumption patterns and decision processes. We have observed three prominent macro trends emerging from these changing behaviors, which are driving the market toward more individualized interactions. The first is the scaling of digital media; the second is the proliferation and penetration of social media; and the third is the multiscreen, always-on mobile population. We will delve more deeply into these trends in Chapter 4, but it's important to note that, as they continue to increase in scale, so will our capacity for addressability—and our commitment to customer centricity and individualized digital experiences across media and channels.

Over the time period of 2010 to 2014, we've seen a marked downward shift in the consumption of traditional media such as radio and print; at the same time, consumers have drastically increased the number of hours spent on digital media, social in particular, with an increase from about 52 minutes a day to nearly 90.[2] In 2010 Google didn't have a social media capability, and today, 540 million people have accounts on Google+.[3] Pinterest is a 300-person company, and one in every four women in the United States is using it on a weekly basis . . . incredible.[4]

Mobile is scaling, too. Today, we've hit an inflection point, where mobile Internet use is actually eclipsing desktop use.[5] Who would have thought that would happen so fast? So the shift is on from traditional media to new media. And marketers are trying to leverage the use of data to figure out to whom—and how—they should offer individualized digital experiences. Advertisers in particular are shifting their dollars into this effort. In response to massive consumer migration to digital, brands are scaling their mobile and social media advertising budgets across formats such as native and video.

All of this digital interaction is creating a tremendous amount of data. Each day, 182 billion emails are sent.[6] Each month, 70 billion pieces of content are shared on Facebook.[7] As Google Executive Chairman Eric Schmidt observed, "There were five exabytes (5 million terabytes) of information created from the dawn of civilization to 2003, but that much information is now created every two days, and the pace is increasing." For one of our top clients, we manage a single database that contains over 8 billion page views and more than 24 terabytes of data for a single brand.

The exhaust coming from all of this digital movement is data. Lots of it. And it's scaling quickly.

---

[2] GfK, "MultiMedia Mentor" as cited by Interactive Advertising Bureau, "45 Million Reasons and Counting to Check Out the New Fronts" conducted in partnership with GfK, April 29, 2013; and Experian, "Experian Marketing Services Reveals 27 Percent of Time Spent Online Is on Social Networking," press release, April 16, 2013.

[3] Ken Yeung, "Two Years Later, Google+ Is Growing, with 540m Active Users Worldwide, 1.5b Photos Uploaded Each Week," *The Next Web, Inc.* (blog), October 29, 2013.

[4] Leslie Meredith, "What Pinterest Reveals about Women," *The Christian Science Monitor* (blog), February 22, 2013.

[5] Tom Standage, "In 2013 the Internet Will Become a Mostly Mobile Medium. Who Will Be the Winners and Losers?" *The Economist*, January 18, 2013.

[6] Sara Radicati and Justin Levenstein, "Email Market, 2013–2017," The Radicati Group, Inc., November 2013.

[7] Statistic Brain, "Social Networking Statistics," January 1, 2014.

To consider addressability in the context of this much data is overwhelming. It simply can't be achieved through traditional methods. Not only is the overall digital media marketplace going to be $61 billion by 2017,[8] but a significant portion of digital media today is, in fact, being bought programmatically, meaning through an automated approach that uses technology to select audiences based on data and analytic insights. Real-time bidding on media is actually going to reach $10.5 billion by 2017,[9] growing more than 50 percent. And we estimate custom audiences, or "identified addressability," to reach the $8 billion mark by that time. So the shift is toward digital but to the individual addressability opportunity within digital as well. As marketers, we're trying to build strategies for first-party and third-party data to aggregate that information so that we can apply analytics to it and deploy on this abundance of digital platforms. Brands—and the marketers charged with driving their growth—cannot keep up with this pace without continually upskilling themselves to capitalize on the massive opportunity. You will make swift progress or you will fall by the wayside while other companies—and other marketing executives with them—pass you by.

The power of addressability to create competitive advantage, both for the organization and for the marketer, has been proven by history. To set up some context, it is meaningful to consider its roots, which are surprisingly deep. We observe, in general, two distinct eras of addressability at scale (see Figure 1.1). Each possesses three common criteria of scale and effectiveness to drive superior performance. The first is individual-level addressability, which goes beyond broad segments, demographics, or panel-level data to reach individuals directly. The second is that the addressable platforms must have massive reach. And third, you must be able to deliver via immersive formats; meaning media and channels that are accessible by the general population. We have found that marketers who tap into the opportunity presented by these three factors have outpaced market growth rates by two to three times and have enjoyed competitive advantage for a sustained period.

With "addressability at scale 1.0," the individual-level addressability factors were limited mostly to name and address—and later phone number. The primary addressable platform at scale was the United States Postal

---

[8] "US Total Media Ad Spend Inches Up, Pushed by Digital Read More," *eMarketer Daily*, August 22, 2013.
[9] Kate Maddox, "Real-time Bidding Pushes Display Advertising to Double-digit Growth," *AdAge BtoB*, November 18, 2013.

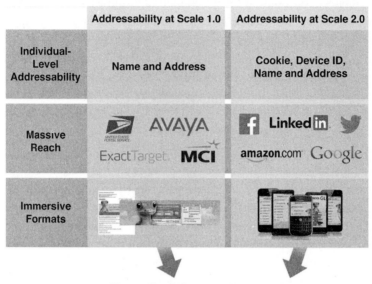

	Addressability at Scale 1.0	Addressability at Scale 2.0
Individual-Level Addressability	Name and Address	Cookie, Device ID, Name and Address
Massive Reach		
Immersive Formats		

Two to three times market growth rate and sustained competitive advantage over 10 years

FIGURE 1.1   Drivers of Scale and Effectiveness

Service (USPS), whose reach was basically 100 percent of the nation's households. The direct mail format allowed for the use of imagery and long-form content in a manner that was highly immersive. There were many different engagement tools that could be delivered on the platform, from direct mail to catalogs. The USPS and third-party providers offered solutions and standards that helped us optimize on the platform, like National Change of Address (NCOA), Delivery Sequence File (DSF), and numerous proprietary tools. Companies figured out how to take both first- and third-party data, deploy analytics to that data, and leverage it using those tools. We became (or hired) experts who lived and breathed the nuances of the USPS platform. We used a framework to help brands create competitive differentiation. For all practical purposes, this was the start of addressability at scale. We helped our clients figure out how to segment their customers and create experiences for them using addressability. We helped them optimize the performance of their marketing programs through accurate measurement. We built technology structures to implement those programs. And effectively, we helped them organize their businesses around the opportunity of addressability at scale.

Companies like Capital One, GEICO, and DirecTV were actually executing addressable strategies, just with a different framework than today's. The winners made marketing advancements like we had never seen before. Capital One, for example, had hundreds of people associated with its database marketing and addressability at scale functions. The company emerged as a clear market leader during the time period of 1995 to 2005 because of its strength in leveraging the USPS platform at scale.

If we look at the big picture, addressability at scale 2.0 has many parallels to 1.0, except they exist in an increasingly digital realm. We still have individual-level addressability; it has just expanded into new forms. Now we're dealing not only with name, address, and phone, but with cookies, mobile device IDs, and social IDs. We have seen the digital audience platforms scale to massive reach with immersive formats in site, search, display, and social media, with new channels such as addressable TV emerging. They are providing us with countless different toolsets and targeting products that we can use to optimize on their platforms. Google alone has given us an integrated addressable platform, inclusive of its own ad network, exchange, server, and, of course, search platform, that delivers addressable experiences across devices and formats, such as YouTube. For Facebook, targeting products include the Facebook Exchange (FBX) and Custom Audiences, which can be optimized through a number of certified third-party partner toolsets. For Twitter, it's products like tailored audiences, keyword targeting, and TV conversation targeting, in which audiences can be purchased directly or through third-party partner toolsets. Numerous unexpected players, including Amazon, eBay, and even Walmart, are following close behind with their own similar offerings. And these behemoth audience platforms have spawned a massive ecosystem of advertising technology, or "ad tech" companies to supply data, targeting, and measurement tools intended to support or enhance addressability. One need only glance at a LUMAscape[10] infographic to imagine the number and complexity of these tools. There are literally thousands of companies that are developing technologies to help us optimize on these platforms.

So, the crucial question is: who is going to take advantage of addressability at scale in 2.0? The opportunity is there, but most of the market is constrained in its ability to scale its addressable spend to make a significant impact. Our belief is that there will be noteworthy winners and

---

[10]   www.lumapartners.com/resource-center/.

losers. Most marketers who are moving their brand spend into more direct, measurable media tools, such as programmatic, performance-based, and direct response, are still working through the traditional marketing funnel. That funnel is narrow, with awareness at the top and little to no addressability. They end up spending marketing resources to contact people they don't know. And often, adverse selection is a problem, where people who don't have a high value potential are the ones cascading down the funnel. This, in turn, presents a targeting dilemma: a small audience of people who can ultimately be converted, wasted remarketing dollars, and a generally less valuable client base. It's only at the bottom of the funnel, after the restricted universe of converted customers comes out, that marketers can have insights about the outcomes of their marketing tactics. The result is a very inefficient funnel that's simply not scalable—all because you started out with no addressability at the top.

Historically, even in the most direct-response-focused industries, budgets have been heavily concentrated on the upper and lower parts of the funnel. One insurance advertiser we know spends more than $700 million in media, with more than 70 percent of that budget going into top-of-funnel tactics, such as television, print, sponsorships, and guaranteed display. This advertiser also spends more than $200 million a year at the very bottom of the funnel on things like branded search, aggregators, ecommerce, and call center experience. All told, this advertiser spends less than 15 percent of its combined consumer budget in the mid-funnel, where consumers actually consider, engage with, and decide which products they will buy from which brand. We call this the "cinched belt" phenomenon. Spend is fat at the top and bottom but cinched tight in the middle. The reason for this has not been a lack of desire to spend more in this area. This insurance marketer would love to find a way to productively spend another $100 million in the mid-funnel.

Until recently, lack of addressability has been the primary constraint to spending in the mid-funnel. Once broad awareness and share of voice were established, little could be done to engage with individual consumers as they moved through consideration and into decision. Direct mail was used to target individuals whom we believed were in-market, but that medium is now in decline. Email and display were used to relentlessly and impersonally retarget with diminishing returns. Once these tactics were maxed out, marketers were out of ideas for how to stay engaged with consumers through the buying process. So they saved their dollars to really unload on the consumer once they typed the brand name into Google or appeared on the site.

Enter the addressable consumer experience. Now the advertiser can take advantage of increased addressability to drive more targeted, timely interactions with the consumer through the key moments of the cycle. A single consumer can be engaged with an individually targeted message in the Facebook newsfeed, receive a personalized offer on the landing page, get remarketed with a relevant search ad, and receive follow-up via an outbound call—all with a singular brand voice and highly engaging content throughout.

Essentially, we can widen the funnel and place addressability at scale at the top by using data and analytics to target and maximize spend against high-value customers and prospects from the outset. First- and third-party audience platforms are enabling not just targeting but delivery of immersive, highly branded content, such as native and video, across devices. This means the traditional separation between right-brain and left-brain thinking around brand versus performance falls away, leaving a more powerful, integrated approach. And there is a cascading effect all the way down the funnel.

Advertisers now have the opportunity to expand the boundaries of the mid-funnel. In effect, if one equates the mid-funnel with the space between mass media awareness and the ecommerce transaction, the marketer's definition of the mid-funnel must expand dramatically, eating into the traditional boundaries of the upper and lower portions of the funnel.

At the upper end, fewer dollars will be allocated to untargeted messaging through things like national television, and more dollars will be allocated into addressable, programmatic tactics meant to drive consideration through relevance, such as addressable TV and programmatic video. At the bottom end, things like A/B testing and offer optimization will get pulled up into the mid-funnel as tactics integrated into the rest of the addressable experience. In essence, addressable and accountable spending has won most of the budget, which is what most advertisers have been seeking. That insurance marketer can now let that belt out several notches, and overall return on ad spend has increased.

This shift will drive greater returns but will require some fundamental changes to both organizations and external supply chains. The expansion of the mid-funnel boundaries requires re-organization of internal functions for most marketers. "Brand" functions that own domain over certain media like display and social from direct marketing organizations no longer make sense. Organization around media (having separate owners for search, email and display) should be questioned.

Similarly, external marketing supply chains with disconnected components where multiple tech platforms and agencies attempt to deliver the integrated mid-funnel in silos will create complexity and insurmountable barriers to the addressable experience. Consolidating the supply chain to fewer, more vertically integrated suppliers and platforms will become the norm.

The knowledge and insights gained as the audience travels through the funnel extends down into the channel, creating a larger universe of people who can now be brought into the funnel and are more likely to convert (Figure 1.2). This ultimately reduces the targeting dilemma, and this is how we scale. The result is more productive customer marketing, characterized by greater conversion rates. More knowledge means more targeted remarketing efforts. More efficient targeting, greater conversion, and more effective remarketing; they all lead to a richer customer portfolio.

Our experience has proven this—in a big way—time and time again. Our clients have been able to increase their addressable impressions by more than 400 percent. In many cases, they have increased their addressable media spend by over 300 percent. Cost of leads and cost of conversions have decreased by as much as 30 and 40 percent, respectively. We have seen remarketing pools increase more than 500 percent. Average lifetime value of acquired customers has increased by more than 60 percent. And these results aren't atypical. They are commonly seen among our clients who take this opportunity seriously. Imagine the competitive advantage over those brands that don't.

THE MECHANICS OF ADDRESSABILITY AT SCALE

Digital Addressability

Digital addressability involves the use of customer data, whether it is anonymous or identified. Figure 1.3 depicts the addressability spectrum, in which anonymous individuals move to partially identified and identified status over time, as the customer relationship expands and data is being collected. And as both the level of knowledge and the level of identification increase, so does the value of the customer.

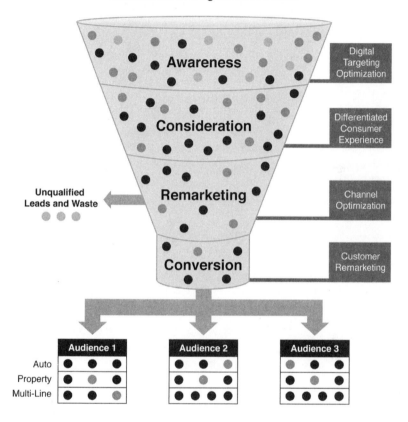

The New Addressable Marketing Funnel

Integrated, targeted management of addressable consumers throughout the funnel

Awareness

Consideration

Remarketing

Conversion

Digital Targeting Optimization

Differentiated Consumer Experience

Channel Optimization

Customer Remarketing

Unqualified Leads and Waste

Audience 1 Audience 2 Audience 3

Auto
Property
Multi-Line

Digital Targeting Optimization
Leverage data and analytics to target and maximize spend on high-value prospects in the addressable universe.

Differentiated Consumer Experience
Leverage addressability to create highly efficient and relevant remarketing experiences.

Channel Optimization
Extension of addressability into channel personalization to drive increased conversion.

Customer Remarketing
Effective utilization of addressability for re-engagement and maximization of existing customers.

FIGURE 1.2   The Evolving Marketing Funnel

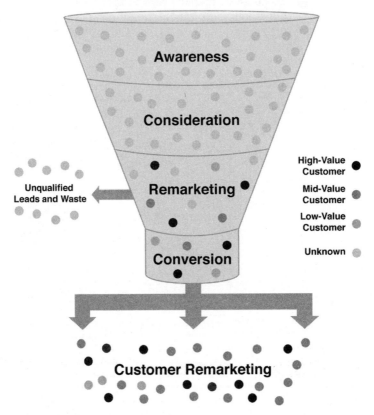

The Marketing Funnel—The Old Way

Awareness
Adverse selection is a big problem in nonaddressable media—"People I don't want are the ones I get to respond."

Consideration
Efficient lead generation but adverse selection from mass and digital media results in lack of scale in quality and, therefore conversion.

Remarketing
Lack of quality and scale of the remarketing pool is bad enough; made worse by an inability to use addressability to engage high-value leads in a relevant experience.

Conversion
As a result, marketers cannot scale budgets due to inefficiencies at the top of the funnel.

FIGURE 1.2 (*Continued*)

Addressability uses customer data (anonymous or identified) to increase the targetability and relevance of marketing impression and experiences.

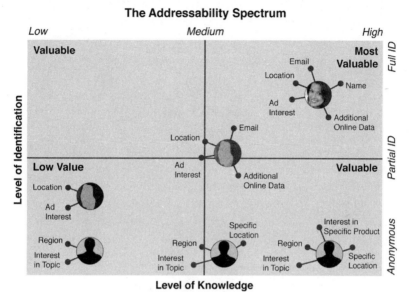

FIGURE 1.3   Addressability Spectrum

Ultimately, the objective is to drive as much content as possible to that most valuable quadrant, where you have as much information on an identified customer as possible. But even in the far right lower quadrant, you will see that, as long as you have individual-level data, you can still drive a lot of value from anonymous consumers.

THE DIGITAL AUDIENCE PLATFORMS

What is enabling that coveted addressability at scale opportunity at the top of the funnel and continuing throughout the funnel, is the growing number and variety of digital audience platforms, which impact the entire funnel. There is an ecosystem in play (Figure 1.4), in which all the members are contributors and benefactors. The consumer wants the speed, relevance, and convenience of digital delivery. The marketer wants high-value customers and prospects. The publisher wants to monetize its audiences. And the platforms themselves are what facilitate the addressability at scale.

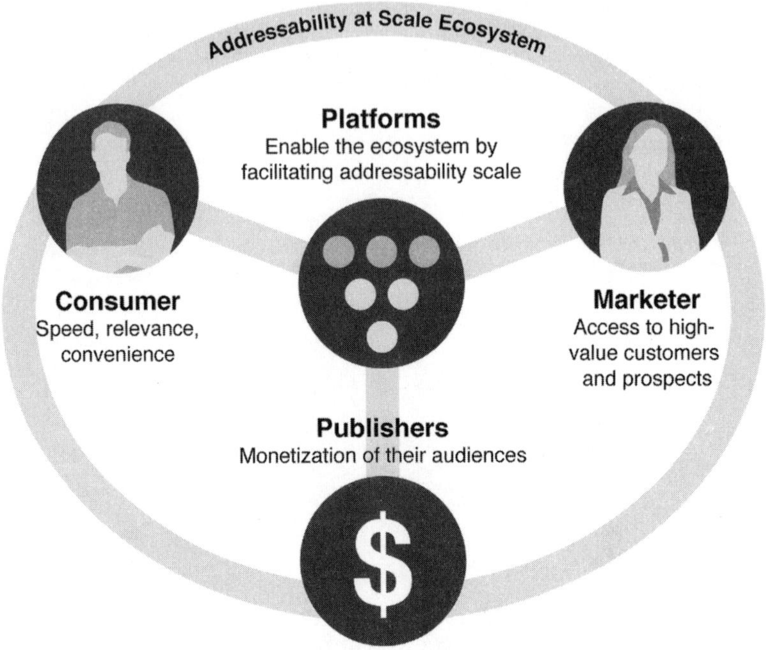

FIGURE 1.4   Addressability at Scale Ecosystem

Historically, marketing planning was focused on which publications would drive performance. As advertisers, the way we bought media was by studying syndicated research panels to determine our targeting demographics, then we went to media publishers to buy our spots, many weeks, even months, in advance. Today, because of digital addressability, our planning is audience based. Where we used to think of quarterly or even annual cycles, we're now using new technologies that are connected to large-scale publishers to carry out individual-level targeting *in real time*. It's less about the up-front plan and more about the ongoing optimization.

If we consider the marketplace and how addressability at scale has evolved from a media perspective, we might look back to the mid-1990s, when we had large audiences who either fit the broad demographics of our target audience, or they didn't see our advertisements (Figure 1.5). Then, in the mid-2000s, we moved to a more contextual, or cohort-based, digital marketing approach, where brands were aggregating audiences of specific interests, and we decided whether those were the interests of our customers

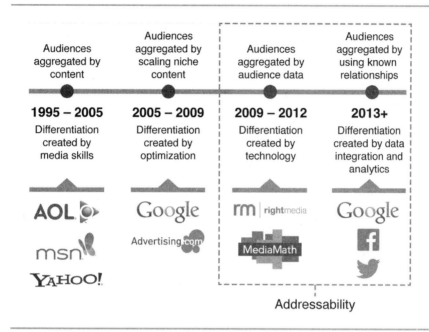

FIGURE 1.5   Evolving Platform Marketplace

or not. A few short years ago, we began to realize there would be value in anonymous customer data. So ad exchanges were developed, and we had the opportunity through those exchanges to use anonymous, individual-level data for targeting.

Now, these audience platforms are creating the opportunity of individual-level targeting, whether anonymous, partially identified, or identified. We define an audience platform as a technology that enables automated, real-time delivery of targeted, personalized experiences to individuals (known and anonymous) at scale utilizing first-party data. One such platform is Facebook and Custom Audiences, where you can take an email address and send it to Facebook and match up to 170 million people in the United States. Another is Twitter, which has been moving forward from cookie-based toward addressable individual-level information as a connection point. Even Google is starting to move its search toward linking to advertisers' first-party data environment to make search ads perform better.

There are many different methods of addressable targeting, such as direct name-and-address match, real-time bidding in the exchanges, intent-based targeting through search platforms, or segment-based targeting coming from other social media companies. Most of these didn't even exist four years ago. The change is happening fast. Most of the different types of digital audience platforms and addressable targeting opportunities didn't exist at all, even four years ago.

And it's happening across devices—PC, mobile, and tablet. It's also happening in search. Many of our clients think of search and say, "Oh, we've been in that space for many years; our plan is working well there." But there has been so much movement in search that they missed while their programs were on auto-pilot. It moved from traditional keyword targeting into different device-based search. And the format is diversifying to include features like video ads and click-to-call. It's now moving into integrated media and targeting, where you can actually load the data that you're collecting back into the platform and begin bidding on media that you would never have in the past, because you now have insights about those consumers.

New audience platforms have begun to arise from unexpected publishers (Figure 1.6). Amazon is now in the space, building a media business that has already reached the $1 billion mark.[11] Even Walmart has recently entered the media business, debuting its own digital marketing platform. And this phenomenon will continue to expand as more and more companies gain these very valuable first-party data assets and look for ways to create new monetization streams. It's just going to increase the opportunity for us all.

To illustrate how dramatically the marketplace is changing, we only need to think back a couple of years. Merkle works with many of the major addressable audience platforms, and we used to suggest that we take their user profile data and combine it with our clients' first- and third-party personally identifiable information (PII). We knew the tremendous potential of analyzing the combined data to determine its value for more robust targeting. The idea met with great resistance from these publishers, who weren't ready to loosen control on their profile data.

But here we are today, with rapid proliferation of addressability, and the use of first-party data on these platforms is the fastest-growing piece of their media business. We're also seeing the rapid build-out of highly integrated tech stacks that enable a lot of this addressability within the publisher platforms. As excited as we were about the prospect of bringing this data together, nobody could have predicted how quickly it would evolve or how broadly it would proliferate.

---

[11] Alistair Barr and Jennifer Saba, "Analysis: Sleeping Ad Giant Amazon Finally Stirs," Reuters.com, April 24, 2013.

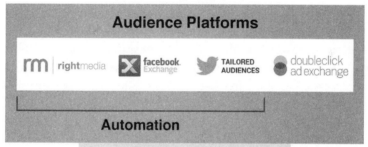

FIGURE 1.6   The Audience Platforms

Whether you're trying to take advantage of the opportunity from the advertising and sales perspective of a publisher or the targeting and reach perspective of an advertiser, it's really hard to keep pace with what's happening. A lot of people think that the targeting is isolated within the audience platforms, as if it's just happening within Facebook or within Google or within Twitter, which have reached scale in and of themselves. But these publishers are all working to extend their ability to reach users off network, which will result in even more massive scale, the likes of which we would never have been able to comprehend before today. They have made some strategic acquisitions, for example: Facebook with Atlas' ad server technology; Google with Dart, DoubleClick, and other tools that enable a single view of the consumer; LinkedIn with Bizo's business audience marketing technology; AOL with marketing optimization platform Convertro; and Twitter with mobile exchange MoPub. These expansions allow the publishers to reach beyond their native environments and start leveraging first-party data to create audience extension networks that enable targeting across a wider landscape outside their platforms. It creates incredible opportunity for addressability at scale, not only for ad targeting but for delivery of rich, meaningful content across devices. The capabilities that the big publishers are creating for first-party data are great within their networks, but they create "walled gardens" that make cross-platform audience management very complex. The "Big 5" publishers—Facebook, Google, Twitter, AOL, and Yahoo!—know this and are adjusting their product and technology strategies accordingly (some more than others).

Today's ever-expanding and highly dynamic digital audience platforms are enabling marketers to scale addressability to unprecedented levels and at record speed. The opportunity is massive, and it's here now, creating a rare opening for brands to seize competitive advantage. It is rapidly changing the marketer's ability to manage the marketing funnel more efficiently and effectively. Taking advantage of this will require a new set of skills, business processes, capabilities and operating models, giving rise to a new breed of marketer who has the competencies to master and implement the integrated data management, technological and execution capabilities, and establish the operating model needed to leverage addressability at scale. This marketer has a deep understanding of CRM principles yet has the knowledge and innovative forethought to thrive in the world of digital audience platforms. We call this new persona *The Platform Marketer*.

THE COMPETENCIES

The Platform Marketer embodies the collective competencies needed to successfully exploit addressability at scale. Those USPS-based competencies that worked in the past were very different from what's required today. To take advantage of the opportunity, new competencies will be required. To succeed as a marketer (and as an organization), you must hone your skills in data, analytics, and audience experience to drive digital performance. You'll need to be a marketing technologist and an expert on the new audience platforms. You'll need to know how to create personalized individual consumer experiences across a multitude of customer touch-points. You'll have to deal with the privacy and compliance hurdles that we face as marketers today. And you must understand measurement and attribution in a much more sophisticated way than you have ever understood it. The brands that leverage these competencies on addressable audience platforms are going to have the greatest opportunity for competitive advantage.

Nine essential competencies lie at the core of platform marketing success: identity management; audience management; consumer privacy and compliance; media optimization; channel optimization; experience design and creation; platform utilization; measurement and attribution; and the technology stack. We have designated a chapter for each of these competencies, as well as the organizational requirements for planning and implementing them. But first, we'll discuss the advent and evolution of the ad tech ecosystem and the digital trends that are driving this new persona.

Chapter 2 The Ad Tech Ecosystem

Special Contributor: Anudit Vikram

We take the Internet for granted. Today we simply assume that any information we may be looking for—an article to read, an article of clothing to wear, a vacation to plan, just about anything—can be found on the Internet. As a matter of fact, many of the details in this chapter have been researched on the Internet. We also assume that most, if not all, of the information we seek and find will be available to us for free. And the reason why we get what we want for free is because publishers that make the content available place advertisements on their pages. These ads help the publishers generate money that allows them to create the content we consume. The systems and processes that play a role in the ad being shown to us comprise the advertising technology (ad tech) ecosystem, which it's not a stretch to say is the major contributor to the ubiquity of the Internet.

ADVERTISING IS AS OLD AS TIME ITSELF

The ancient Egyptians carved public notices in stone as far back as 2000 B.C. In 1472, the first print ad was created in England announcing a prayer book for sale. Product branding came into being with the copy developed for Dentrifice Tooth Gel in 1661. The birth of the automobile gave rise to the billboard in 1835, and the first electric sign went up in Times Square in 1882. Radio advertising began in the 1920s and the first TV commercial ran in 1941.[1]

In this 4,000-year journey, more than 500 years after the beginning of modern advertising and almost 50 years after the advent of TV ads, we saw the beginning of the digital advertising revolution. In 1994, magazine site, Hotwired, launched the first banner ad from AT&T, Sprint, and some others—and we haven't looked back since.

DIGITAL ADVERTISING IS CATCHING UP FAST

In 2013, approximately one quarter of all advertising dollars in the United States were spent on digital advertising.[2] Clocking in at $42.8 billion,[3] digital ad revenues amount to approximately $11.4 billion more than newspapers and magazines combined. It is 57 percent of what was spent on TV advertising ($74.5 billion), but after giving TV a 50-year head start, digital marketing revenues are expected to reach $74.1 billion in 2017, catching up with TV ($75.98 billion).[4] The worldwide market for digital advertising, according to PricewaterhouseCoopers, will reach $185 billion by 2017.[5]

BUT WHAT REALLY IS THIS AD TECH ECOSYSTEM, AND HOW DID IT COME ABOUT?

Powering these billions of dollars are the intricate advertising technology systems that live within the broader technology ecosystem. These technologies are required because advertising on the Internet is a completely different game than any other kind of advertising we have known

---

[1] http://mashable.com/2011/12/26/history-advertising/.
[2] www.iab.net/media/file/IAB_Internet_Advertising_Revenue_Report_FY_2013.pdf.
[3] Ibid.
[4] www.emarketer.com/Article/Total-US-Ad-Spending-See-Largest-Increase-Since-2004/1010982.
[5] www.pwc.com/outlook.

heretofore. While the Internet gives us access to an unlimited audience at a global scale, this audience is also extremely fragmented. Gone are the old methods of advertising based on magazine readership or TV viewership. The consumers browsing the Internet are more independent, more unique, and have the ability to instantly leave their engagement with the advertiser by browsing away from the platforms on which the advertiser is displaying an ad to them. But this very same fickle audience is also very responsive if engaged properly, and their responsiveness can be measured. Today, we are able to break down consumers to the individual level and run campaigns targeted specifically to them. We can further analyze exactly what is working and what is not and take remedial actions appropriately. This segmentation, targeting, and measurement of our digital advertising spend is enabled by the ad tech ecosystem.

THE BIG PICTURE

Before we get to the details of this ecosystem, let us start by looking at the big picture. Terence Kawaja, founder and CEO of LUMA Partners LLC, gave a presentation in 2010, where he presented the slide shown in Figure 2.1.[6]

As you can see, it is a complex web of technologies that plays a role in getting the right ad in front of you. To better understand exactly what role these technologies play and how they play them, let us look at what happens when you access a digital property.

Let's say that you were on the Internet one evening looking to buy a new laptop. You browsed some websites, searched for laptops and studied a few, even put one in your cart at Amazon. But you got distracted before you finished a purchase and went to sleep. The next day, you wake up to check the news and notice that there is an ad from Amazon among the headlines on the website. This ad shows you laptops and maybe even the exact same laptop you had abandoned in your cart. How did this happen? How did Amazon know you would be at this website and manage to buy an ad space there showing you the exact same laptop you had been looking at just a few hours ago? An intricate dance using members of the

---

[6] Picture source at: www.lumapartners.com/lumascapes/display-ad-tech-lumascape/.

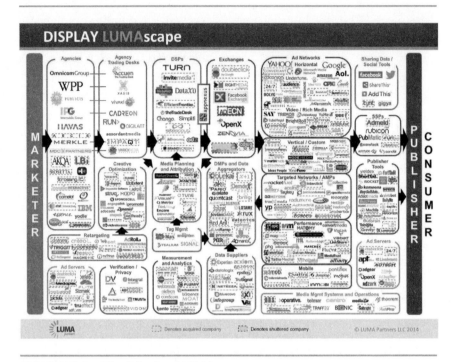

FIGURE 2.1 The Display LUMAscape

chart in Figure 2.1 was responsible for you seeing what you saw. Figure 2.2 depicts how it plays out.

When you browse a website (1), the site's web server returns a bunch of code (2) telling the browser what to display. Within this code is a link, known as an ad tag. In its simplest form, the ad tag points to the publisher's ad server (3), which looks inside itself to decide what ad to show. The server then returns that ad to the browser (4) for you to see, and the process ends (we will ignore the third-party buyer ad server call for now). But more likely, the publisher's ad server returns some code that points to what is called a supply-side platform (SSP) (5). The browser now calls the SSP (6), which then starts what is called an auction on its own side (7), reaching out to and requesting bids from a number of demand sources. These demand sources could be demand-side platforms (DSP) and/or ad networks (8). The DSPs and ad networks look within their own sets of buyer relationships to find which ad they want to show to the user and how much they want to pay for it. DSPs may run another auction on their side (9) to decide the most relevant ad and bid. The DSPs and ad networks then submit a bid (10) back to the SSP. The SSP executes an auction to find the highest-paying ad

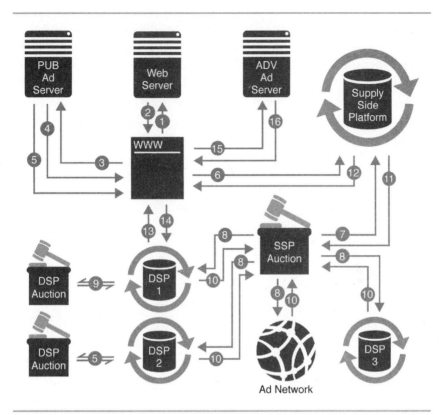

FIGURE 2.2   Anatomy of an Ad Call

(11) and passes it back to the browser (12). The code passed back to the browser essentially functions as a redirect, and the browser now calls the winning DSP directly (13). The DSP sends back the code containing the ad it wants to show (14). The code is a redirect to the marketer's ad server and the browser then calls the ad server (15). The ad server returns the actual creative and the ad is shown (16).

UNDERSTANDING THE PLAYERS

Now that we have seen how this all plays out, let's look at each of the pieces of the puzzle in a little more detail. From a user-centric viewpoint, the first interaction with the ad tech ecosystem comes at the publisher site.

A *publisher* is any business, individual, or organization that prepares and issues or delivers content to an audience. Publishers may not actually create all the content. Some websites or online magazines, for example, buy content from elsewhere for publishing. In many cases, the publisher acts as a host, or medium, for the content, and there are many cases where advertising is placed around that content.[7] Examples of publishers are entities like Gannett and Hearst; known brands like NBC, CNN, and CBS; and portals such as Yahoo!, MSN, and AOL. These publishers create their own content or syndicate it from others to present to users coming to their sites. Social sites such as Facebook, Twitter, Pinterest, and LinkedIn are examples of publishers where content is generated by the users who visit these sites. The business model that generates revenue through the placement of ads is the genesis of the ad tech ecosystem.

While the user may not explicitly see it, the next piece of the ecosystem that he or she touches is the ad server.

An *ad server* is a web-based tool used by publishers, networks, and advertisers to help with ad management, campaign management, and ad trafficking. An ad server also provides reporting on ads served on the website. Finally, an ad server serves the creative side; this means that the ad server or ad serving company also delivers the ad to each user's browser.[8] As you would have noted in the diagram in Figure 2.2 and the description in the prior section, there are two types of ad servers: a publisher (or seller) side ad server and a marketer (or buyer) side ad server.

Publisher ad servers like DoubleClick for Publishers (DFP) or Open Ad Stream (OAS) are systems that work on behalf of a publisher. They help publishers manage their advertising campaigns and report on them, allowing publishers to generate and recognize revenue from their web properties. DoubleClick for Advertisers (DFA), now called DoubleClick Campaign Manager (DCM), Atlas, MediaPlex, and Sizmek are examples of *advertiser ad servers*. They host and serve the creative treatments that advertisers want to show their users and are the systems that the advertisers use as the source of truth when it comes to billing and financial aspects of their media transactions with publishers.

The crux of the workflow is this: The advertiser's ad from the advertiser ad server is being shown to the user on a publisher site via the publisher ad server. But this simple flow has a very complex middle layer with players that include *ad networks*.

---

[7] www.quora.com/What-is-an-online-publisher-What-is-a-content-provider.
[8] www.zedo.com/what-is-ad-server/.

Ad networks arose because the supply and demand equation on the Internet is not as easily quantifiable as in other media. With newspapers and magazines you know exactly how many copies you have printed and your circulation reach, and thus you can estimate how many times you will expose a certain ad. With TV, you know the population of the area in which your programs are broadcasting, and thus you can predict the potential number of people who might view a certain ad. But when it comes to the Internet two complications come into play.

From the seller (publisher) side, traffic to the websites is not a constant. Depending on a myriad of factors, the same website may see a few users one day and many more the next. (As an example, a weather website may see minimal traffic when the weather is normal and stable and then a deluge of users visit if a storm suddenly hits or weather advisories are issued). This means that publishers will likely end up with instances when the number of ads they have sold is less than the traffic they see on their sites and, thus, they lose out on potential revenue they could have generated because ad space went unsold. Further, some publishers (especially the smaller ones) may not have sales teams big enough to sell out their entire inventory.

From the buyer (advertiser) side, the fragmentation of content on the Internet means that the effort to find the right type of content on which to run their ads is a more expensive exercise. When you buy an ad in magazines like *Cosmopolitan* or *Vogue* or *The Economist* or *Time*, or on TV in shows like *60 Minutes* or *The Walking Dead*, you—as an advertiser—can be relatively certain of the type of content that appears in those magazines or on those TV shows and the type of people who will be consuming that content. But when it comes to Internet publishers, other than the very large brands, finding the right content and audience is a much more complex exercise. Hence, the advent of the ad network.

An ad network is an online business that specializes in matching advertisers to websites looking to host advertisements. Advertising networks work as brokers for both suppliers (sites with content that can host ads) and buyers (the advertisers).[9]

Some examples of ad networks are Tribal Fusion, Specific Media, Media.net, and Conversant.

The business model for ad networks is one of arbitrage, where the network makes money by pocketing the difference between what they pay to buy the

---

[9] www.techopedia.com/definition/26590/advertising-network-ad-network.

inventory from the publisher and the price at which they sell it to the advertiser. This model results in a loss of transparency to the publisher and the advertiser and is sometimes not acceptable to them. A further problem with first-generation ad networks was that when the networks could not monetize the inventory they had already bought, they resold it to other networks to try and recoup their investment. This meant that there were times when an ad impression bounced around from network to network before it was eventually monetized—and by that time its value was almost useless to the advertiser and generated negligible revenue for the publisher. Systems were designed to overcome this challenge and they were called *ad exchanges*.

Ad exchanges are very similar to ad networks in that they comprise a marketplace where buyers and sellers come together. The basic difference between the two is that the exchange business model is more transparent, and the buyer and the seller have full view into the full value of the inventory being transacted. As a matter of fact, exchanges may even have ad networks supplying inventory to the exchange marketplace for advertisers to buy.[10] Popular exchanges are Google Ad Exchange, Yahoo Ad Platform, and Microsoft Advertising Exchange. These three Internet behemoths built their exchanges by buying out pioneers in the online advertising space. Yahoo! acquired Right Media in April 2007 for $680 million,[11] Google bought DoubleClick in May 2007 for $3.1 billion[12] (yes—that's billion with a B!), and Microsoft bought a company called AdECN[13] in July 2007 for an undisclosed amount.[14]

Right Media was the pioneer in the ad exchange space. Right Media started as an ad network in 2003, but by 2006, it had realized that the mess of redirects (ad networks redirecting to other ad networks) and the resulting inefficiencies needed to be fixed. An ad exchange allows the seller to auction its inventory to the highest bidder through a single redirect. The biggest advantage this offers is the transparency that comes with this

---

[10] http://adage.com/article/special-report-ad-network-exchange-guide-2010/ad-networks-exchanges-101/143310/.

[11] http://techcrunch.com/2007/04/29/panama-not-enough-to-battle-google-yahoo-acquires-rightmedia/.

[12] www.nytimes.com/2007/04/14/technology/14DoubleClick.html.

[13] www.marketwatch.com/story/microsoft-buys-online-ad-exchange-adecn-inc.

[14] I wanted to list these numbers just to give you, the reader, an idea as to how much the exchanges changed the online media world. The Big Three—Google, Microsoft, and Yahoo!—were holding nothing back to get into the game and get into it fast!

method of monetization and enhanced access to inventory. This greatly increases efficiency for both publishers and advertisers.

As the market matured, advertisers came to demand more specialized technologies that were focused solely on the buy-side interests (as opposed to the typical networks and exchanges, which worked both the sell-side and the buy-side). This gave birth to the demand-side platform (DSP).

Demand-side platforms are technological systems used to purchase advertising in an automated fashion.[15] They allow advertisers to buy impressions across a range of publisher sites. DSPs use information such as location and behavioral preferences to decide which impressions make the most sense for an advertiser to buy and determine the right price to pay for those impressions. This price is determined in a real-time auction using a technology called real-time bidding (RTB) and eliminates the need for human negotiation, since the impressions are simply auctioned to the highest bidder.[16]

DSPs work on behalf of the advertiser and provide transparency and control to the advertiser, allowing maximized return on ad spend (ROAS). A good DSP maintains relationships with many supply sources through networks and exchanges. The DSP makes that inventory available to the advertiser, always working to help buy the inventory at the best possible price. DataXu, MediaMath, and Turn are some of the better known DSPs in the market today.

Digressing a little from the LUMAScape, a note about RTB is paramount when discussing online advertising. This is the technology that has been responsible for radical changes in the way media is bought and sold. Before the advent of RTB, media transactions required that the seller make the inventory available and specify its attributes and that the buyer make a predetermined offer for a given inventory depending on its attributes. Three situations resulted.

1. Inventory value was predetermined (buyers decided what price they wanted to pay for a certain URL, or context, and when that inventory came up for sale, the price was paid).
2. Price optimization, if carried out, was done in an offline manner and new prices were then preloaded. Buyers looked at performance metrics to see what was working and what was not and manually changed the price they wanted to pay for inventory based on their analysis.

---

[15] http://digiday.com/platforms/wtf-demand-side-platform/.
[16] Ibid.

3. Discrepancies in inventory categorization came to light only post-campaign, too late for the advertiser to do anything about it. A buyer thought he was buying a user on a news site, but miscategorization meant the inventory was actually from a sports site. The buyer would find out about this only in post-campaign reporting and would have to ask for adjustments. A sports site instead of a news site may not be too far off base, but what if it was a porn site instead of the expected news site? Even if the buyer does get a post-campaign adjustment, the potential harm to the brand has already been done.

Real-time bidding changed all that. With the advent of RTB, technology advertisers (working through DSPs) were able to see—in real time—attributes of the user while on the page and decide how valuable that user was to them. An appropriate bid was placed for the impression, taking into account all the attributes that were available to use. For example, Zappos might recognize that a user has previously been on its site looking at a specific pair of shoes, and therefore might be prepared to pay more than Amazon or Best Buy to serve ads to her. The price of impressions is determined in real time, based on what buyers are willing to pay, hence the name "real-time bidding."[17]

Now that we understand what the RTB technology is all about, let us come back to the platform that uses this technology.

With the proliferation of the DSPs, the ad tech scales had started to tilt in favor of the advertiser. Advertisers had technology platforms working for them and the publishers needed an advocate in their corner as well. This was the reason for the development of the supply-side platform (SSP).

Supply-side platforms are the publisher equivalent of the DSP (Figure 2.3).[18] Just as the DSPs are used by advertisers to buy inventory as cheaply as possible, the SSPs are used by publishers to maximize the revenue they can generate from their properties. They do this by connecting publishers to as many demand sources as possible, thus increasing the possible demand for their inventory and driving the best possible rates.[19]

SSPs work on behalf of the publisher. In addition to opening up their inventory they also give publishers control mechanisms, such as the ability to set price floors and decide which advertisers or channels they want to

---

[17] http://digiday.com/platforms/what-is-real-time-bidding/.
[18] http://digiday.com/platforms/wtf-supply-side-platform/.
[19] Ibid.

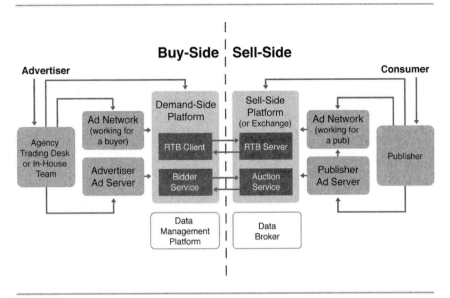

FIGURE 2.3   Buy-Side versus Sell-Side Platforms

have access to their inventory and at what price.[20] Pubmatic and Rubicon are two of the better known SSPs that are helping publishers realize their revenue goals. In addition to the platforms already discussed, there is another piece of technology that is of great importance in today's advertising workflows: the data management platform (DMP).

Today's marketing ecosystem is all about being able to find the right consumer at the right time in the right place. The right time and the right place are handled using RTB technology, but finding the right consumer means having some way to organize and collect information about the users in an efficient, privacy-sensitive, and regulatory-compliant manner—and then being able to effectively use that information when buying media.

A *data management platform* is a centralized technology system that allows you to create target audiences based on a combination of in-depth first-party and third-party audience data, accurately target campaigns to these audiences across third-party ad networks and exchanges, and measure with accuracy which campaigns performed the best across segments and channels to refine media buys and ad creative over time.[21]

---

[20] Ibid.

[21] www.bluekai.com/data-management-platform.php.

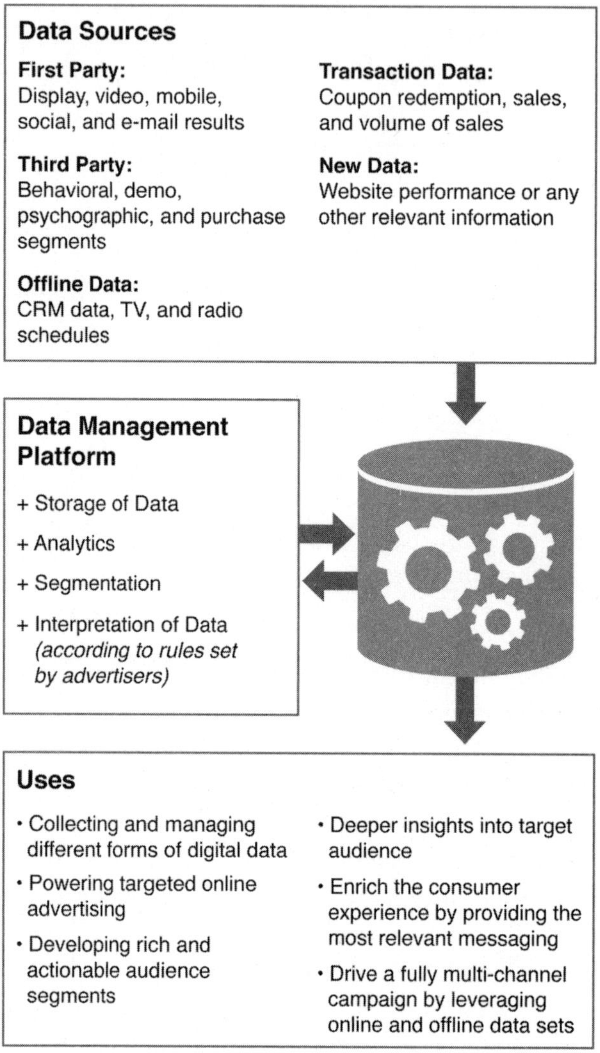

Data Sources

First Party:
Display, video, mobile, social, and e-mail results

Transaction Data:
Coupon redemption, sales, and volume of sales

Third Party:
Behavioral, demo, psychographic, and purchase segments

New Data:
Website performance or any other relevant information

Offline Data:
CRM data, TV, and radio schedules

Data Management Platform

+ Storage of Data

+ Analytics

+ Segmentation

+ Interpretation of Data
(according to rules set by advertisers)

Uses

• Collecting and managing different forms of digital data

• Powering targeted online advertising

• Developing rich and actionable audience segments

• Deeper insights into target audience

• Enrich the consumer experience by providing the most relevant messaging

• Drive a fully multi-channel campaign by leveraging online and offline data sets

FIGURE 2.4   DMP Sources and Uses

In the simplest of senses, a DMP is a real-time database that allows you to collect first-, second-, and third-party data across different channels, analyze and visualize it to understand performance and other business metrics, and further syndicate it to downstream systems to affect your marketing programs (Figure 2.4).

The DMP is also the foundational platform that allows you to put the data to interesting business uses. The DMP can feed into decisioning and personalization engines to enable you to have individualized conversations with your customer. The data in the DMP can help generate insights and drive models for attribution to help you get a better understanding of what is working and what is not as you engage in complex marketing programs. In short, the DMP is a repository, a platform that allows you to have a unified, holistic view of your most prized asset—your data.

Advertiser-side DMPs allow advertisers to make more informed and targeted buys, ensuring that their messages are reaching exactly the type of users they want exposed. Publisher-side DMPs allow publishers to collect information about site visitors and bundle this newly created data asset with their inventory. This lets them charge premium prices for their inventory, because advertisers are now privy to more information about the media buy than they would have been without this data.

All these platforms working together make it possible for you to see the ad you saw when you browsed the Internet just a little while ago. But, as you can imagine, making the most effective use of these platforms—while absolutely necessary for the successful and efficient running of online marketing campaigns—is not an easy task.

THE IMPORTANCE OF DATA IN ONLINE ADVERTISING

Now that we've studied the data management platforms, a discussion of the impact of data in this ecosystem will help you fully understand the coming changes in the way media plans are being executed. Earlier in the chapter, we discussed real-time bidding and the advantages it provides by automating auctions and facilitating ways to determine the appropriate value of an impression. But these advantages would be meaningless without the data attributes associated with each impression.

An RTB system by itself would not know anything about the impression and, hence, would not be able to assign any value to it. It is the data associated with the impression that lets the RTB algorithm determine its value. RTB has brought the speed of automation to pricing and serving the ad, but it is the data that has brought the precision and individualization to targeting, making digital buys so much more effective.

The types of data collected can be very diverse, and the uses of this data are myriad. We can study *technographic* data that is exposed by the

FIGURE 2.5   The User Data Ecosystem Map*

*Replicated by BlueKai in logo format.

Source: Adapted with permission from BCG Perspectives, "The Evolution of Online-User Data," Report, January 2012.

browsers and the devices being used, *geographic* data by parsing out the IP address from which the user is coming, *contextual* data as gleaned from the content of the page, or *intent* data as gathered from users' search terms and keywords. But the most interesting and widely used of all the data types—and the one that is responsible for the ability to target a specific type of individual for a specific marketing campaign—is what is known as *behavioral* data. This data type makes audience targeting possible and online advertising so much more effective. Behavioral targeting is said to be more than twice as effective as non-behaviorally targeted advertising.[22]

In the early days of digital advertising, advertisers used sites as a proxy for audience. If you wanted to target men, you advertised on ESPN.com. But as technology matured, it became possible to keep track of these users as they moved around the Internet. You could, in theory, find men even when they were not on ESPN.com because they had been to ESPN.com at some time in the past and you tracked them from there on. Nowadays,

---

[22] www.networkadvertising.org/pdfs/Beales_NAI_Study.pdf.

vendors known as data providers capture this browsing behavior data across Internet sites, package it, and sell it to advertisers that use it to target users in their campaigns (Figure 2.5). The data ecosystem is almost as complicated as the digital marketing LUMAScape itself![23]

The net effect of collecting this immense variety of data and making inferences from it is the increased complexity in data packaging and its use. Audiences can now be sliced and diced in so many specific and complex ways that you can sabotage your results by targeting so precisely that the number of individuals you end up with is too small to run an effective campaign against.

If used properly, data can work wonders for an online campaign, but if left unchecked or in the hands of someone inexperienced, it can wreck a campaign. How the data affects your campaign is a function of how you use it, but what is always true now is that there is another intermediary—the data vendor—who plays an important role in your ad operations workflow.

THE WAY THE MONEY FLOWS

With an understanding of the players in this ecosystem and how they work together, we need to focus on the root objective of all this. Or, in the words of Jerry Maguire's client, Rod Tidwell, "Show me the money!"

While each of these players performs a role that is critical for the end-to-end functioning of our media plans, the reality is that putting so many intermediaries in play causes erosion in the economics of the system. According to one accepted analysis,[24] of every $5.00 that is spent by an advertiser, the publisher—on whose property the ad is shown—only realizes about $1.80. Why is this?

In the early days, the days of less complex systems, advertisers would use an agency to buy from a publisher. The costs in this workflow were the fees charged by the agency and that was pretty much it. (We'll ignore the technology cost of the ad servers on the publisher and the advertiser side since they are essentially working directly for the publisher and the advertiser

---

[23] www.rtbchina.com/wp-content/uploads/2012/02/User-Data-Ecosystem.png.
[24] www.slideshare.net/tkawaja/terence-kawajas-iab-networks-and-exchanges-keynote.

and are, therefore, not added costs.) If the agency charged a 10 percent agency fee, the publisher would receive $4.50 for each $5.00 spent.

As the complexity increased with the advent of ad networks, intermediaries came into play. The ad networks now took a piece of the pie, as did some of the other services that came along with the networks—services like campaign analytics. (Now that you had the intermediaries, you needed other intermediaries to help you track the spend across the intermediaries!) Of the advertiser's initial $5.00 spend, $0.50 went to the agency (the 10 percent agency fee), the ad networks kept about $2.00, and the tech fee for the intermediaries would account for another $0.10 or so. The publisher now recognized $2.40 of the $5.00 spent by the advertiser.

And then we made it even more complex with the DSPs, the exchanges, the SSPs, and, if you look at the LUMAScape diagram, you'll see the creative optimizers, the data providers, the ad verification companies, and so on. Even the simplest of this complex workflow now had multiple intermediaries in play. The publisher payout began to look something like the diagram in Figure 2.6.

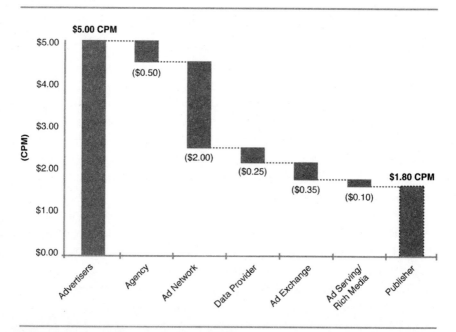

FIGURE 2.6   Ad Revenue Breakdowns
Source: www.slideshare.net/tkawaja/terence-kawajas-iab-networks-and-exchanges-keynote.

In this chapter, we called out only the very few boxes from the LUMAScape diagram in Figure 2.1 that we feel are critical to the online advertising workflow. A full detail of these featured boxes, and even a partial discussion of all the LUMAScape boxes, would be a book in itself!

The point to note is that today's marketer must understand these platforms and know how—and in what combination—to use them. It's at the heart of becoming a Platform Marketer.

Chapter 3   Introducing the Platform Marketer

To take advantage of these new and constantly changing audience platforms and to create clear differentiation among a sea of competitors, brands must create an ongoing and relevant dialogue with their customers. It becomes exceedingly difficult with the continued proliferation of inbound digital consumer-to-brand channels (such as websites and call centers), outbound digital brand-to-consumer media (such as display advertising and email), and the platforms themselves. Brands are developing a new array of skills, tools, processes, and metrics; and they are building or acquiring the expertise to implement these capabilities in their day-to-day engagements with consumers. This is imperative for the survival of any customer-centric organization, as the environment becomes more and more competitive. Indeed, it is imperative for the Platform Marketer himself to develop these skills. Due to the increased complexity of leveraging data, technology, and analytics in this new era, the brands that capitalize on addressability at scale will create more enduring and sustained competitive advantage.

As we touched on in Chapter 1, the Platform Marketer embodies a collection of competencies that are required to take advantage of addressability at scale. Those USPS-based Platform Marketer competencies that worked in the past have similarities but also significant differences from what's required now. Today's digital marketplace calls for a marketing technologist who is also an expert on the new audience platforms. You'll need to know how to create personalized individual consumer experiences across a multitude of customer touchpoints. You'll have to understand and comply with the privacy hurdles that we face as marketers today. And you must comprehend measurement and attribution in a much more sophisticated way than ever before. The brands that leverage these competencies on the addressable audience platforms, using a proven framework like Connected CRM (cCRM), are going to have a great opportunity for competitive advantage. And so will the marketing professionals themselves.

Nine essential competencies lie at the core of platform marketing success: identity management, audience management, consumer privacy and compliance, media optimization, channel optimization, experience design and creation, platform utilization, measurement and attribution, and the technology stack. They can be categorized into three groups, as depicted in Figure 3.1. These competencies are introduced in the following pages. The remaining chapters in this book are devoted to exploring them in more

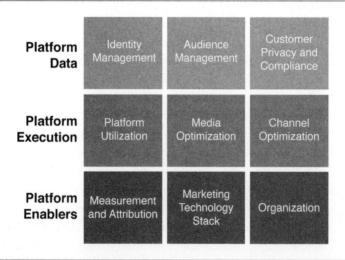

FIGURE 3.1 Platform Marketing Competency Matrix

detail and to helping you hone your skills in data, analytics, and audience experience to drive digital performance across the addressable universe.

IDENTITY MANAGEMENT

Identity management begins with creating a unique consumer identity map for each customer or prospect across media and channels. This identity map is updated on an ongoing basis as consumer engagements create new identity connections. Identity currencies are those customer identifiers, anonymous and known, that allow for effective analysis and targeting. These include such features as physical name and address, email address, mobile number, customer IDs, social handles, probabilistic IDs, and cookies. A single persistent "key" or identity is created when these currencies are linked and merged together. In turn, all anonymous and known digital interactions are aggregated at the individual level into a singular event stream for targeting, personalization, measurement, and insights.

Effective identity management maximizes the collection of consumer addressability data through the development of compelling experiences that incent consumers to provide identification criteria while also making intelligent use of third-party data to enhance customer profiles. It also involves proactively engineering data capture within media and channel to ensure that valuable identity data is retained and connected.

Best practices call for a pervasive identity management capability that provides an integrated view of offline and online channel and media interactions across the organization. This competency ensures that consumer identity and knowledge are maximized. In order to ensure enterprise integration, identity management must be a C-level mandate, owned by executive leadership, with clear metrics for success.

AUDIENCE MANAGEMENT

Audience management builds on identity management through the aggregation of consumer data from multiple sources for the purpose of creating and analyzing consumer profiles or segments. It entails the merging of personally identifiable information (PII) with anonymous data sources in privacy-sensitive ways and the development of segments that can be acted on across identity currencies. These segments can be used for analytic insight purposes and can also be directly syndicated across media and channels in real time to enable targeted communications.

The foundational requirement for effective audience management is the seamless integration of consumer data across offline and online touchpoints. This includes bringing together key consumer currencies, such as name and address, email, cookie ID, and social handle along with audience attributes and behavior. Profiles are built on this data allowing the information to be readily digested and acted on by marketers. An important requirement for effective audience management is the ability to update audience profiles in real time as the consumer is engaging with the organization. Also important is the ability to push segment data, based on any of the consumer currencies, to the appropriate audience platforms in real time and to pull, by facilitating the real-time lookup of segment data, as required.

In this way data might be pushed into audience platforms such as Facebook or the email service provider for outbound communications. It can also be pulled by customer service reps who are in active dialogues with the consumer or pulled into a decision engine for real-time targeting on a website.

CONSUMER PRIVACY AND COMPLIANCE

With increasing attention being paid to the collection and use of consumer data, the Platform Marketer must be a vigilant and responsible steward of that information.

Scrutiny, from legislative and regulatory entities as well as privacy advocates, requires marketers to constantly monitor and participate in the shaping of consumer privacy regulations and industry requirements. These efforts are critical to the proactive development of enterprise-level consumer data protection standards. The objective is to create data practices that strike a balance among the needs and expectations of the business, the industry, and the consumer, while enabling innovation and value creation.

Supporting these efforts is a consistent, clear, and effective communication plan across the organization, designed to educate and promote the values of a robust consumer privacy program. Additionally, your consumer data collection efforts should reflect your commitment to the integrity and protection of the data from corruption and/or unauthorized access or breach. As we know, a strong and robust privacy program can be undermined very quickly if sufficient focus is not paid to how and where data is stored, who can access it, and how unauthorized access can be detected (if not in all cases prevented).

MEDIA OPTIMIZATION

While identity and audience management create data and insight "fuel," the engine that drives addressability at scale is the combination of competencies and assets within media and channel optimization. Within the world of media, new competencies in addressable media planning, programmatic media buying, and buy optimization have arisen that take full advantage of the scaling addressability in the audience platforms.

Gone are the days of the traditional "mad men" approach, where relationships and intuition drove the media plan and buy. The media optimization expert in today's marketplace uses a consolidated data view of the customer. That view is housed in an integrated media platform that manages a complex web of programmatic media buying and optimization tactics throughout the marketing funnel, including programmatic guaranteed, exchange-based, and direct-match tactics that have become hallmark tactics of the Platform Marketer.

This is a blend of the art of platform optimization and the science of machine learning and automation. All of this is managed through an audience-based (rather than publisher-based), addressable media plan.

CHANNEL OPTIMIZATION

Channel optimization is the process by which a company leverages data to manage and improve the channel to enhance customer experiences, increase interactions, and drive an increase in incremental conversions. Channel optimization focuses on incremental improvements to the consumer's experience, in order to drive high-value engagements between the brand and the consumer.

As in the realm of media optimization, within the world of the digital channel, new competencies have arisen to take advantage of the increasing addressability of the decision management and content management capabilities within the domain of the first-party audience platform (example: your website). These include real-time personalization as well as experience planning and execution. The media and channel optimization disciplines are highly interrelated and must be expertly integrated with an overarching experience planning and execution discipline that considers the overall experience, from the first ad impression through to customer loyalty.

EXPERIENCE DESIGN AND CREATION

The Platform Marketer has mastered the intersection of creative with data and analytics in the evolving digital platforms, and across media and channel, to create a data-driven customer journey. There are three core creative capabilities to be mastered, and they all require a change in traditional creative culture.

1. A dedicated team of creative rock stars, well-versed in new media platforms, including Twitter and Facebook, are aggressively innovating in new advertising formats.

    The Platform Marketer knows that these emerging advertising platforms demand a different type of creative team. This dedicated team is able to produce new creative twice a week instead of twice a year. The creative is constantly being optimized as a result of instant feedback from the data and analytics provided.

2. A creative team culture purpose-built for one-to-one personalized experiences across all device types.

    Personalization technology has come of age. No two customers will see the same version of your website or mobile website.

    The Platform Marketer knows that the culture established in the creative teams must ensure that creative assets are generated for all different screen sizes at all different segments. Gone are the days that the one-size-fits-all "big idea" image dominates the home page. The creative team is generating 40 to 50 creative assets for a single home page image to be delivered to the right segment on the right device.

3. Truly data-driven customer journeys.

    The Platform Marketer understands that experiences don't start and stop at each channel. The attributes collected against an individual and acted upon on the website should be easily visible across channels such as the call center and mobile app. Truly data-driven customer journeys need to be crafted to ensure that a consumer sees the same, consistent one-to-one personalized brand experience across all channels.

PLATFORM UTILIZATION

We've discussed how the digital audience platforms are creating address-ability at scale through their ability to reach practically everyone, practically all the time. The largest platforms of today, which are gaining scale and momentum all the time, are Google, Twitter, and Facebook, even Pinterest and LinkedIn. But we see enormous potential in the emerging platforms, like AOL, eBay, and Amazon, which are beginning to hold their own among the giants. And every day, third-tier players are entering the market with massive platform opportunities—imagine the content-rich, personalized experiences that can be enabled by platforms like Apple and Walmart, given their customer reach and intimate purchase knowledge. The potential exists for thousands of platforms to arise, and brands will need to figure out how to leverage them for more appropriate engagements with their customers.

Evolution within the platform market is constant. New publishers are entering the market and raising the bar for existing publishers. All are racing to provide greater value to advertisers, who are who are pumping more dollars—and an increasing portion of the marketing budget—into the digital space. The Platform Marketer must face the challenge of keeping up with the pace of change, always staying on top of the changes and advancements that are taking place on the existing and emerging platforms.

MEASUREMENT AND ATTRIBUTION

For the Platform Marketer, effective measurement and attribution are more important than ever before. They involve the development and ongoing management of key performance indicators (KPIs) and underlying methodologies that measure marketing effectiveness and provide insights for agile, ongoing execution. Measurement and attribution requires the development and implementation of an approach that crosses media, channel, and device type and enables fractional attribution, rather than the inaccurate "last-touch" attribution. It also includes tools for visualization and socialization of results and insights.

Today's best practices include KPIs that are consistent, complete, and published across the enterprise with one best estimation method for each metric. Top-down marketing mix models that allocate spend across media integrated with bottom-up, customer-level attribution modeling across direct and digital media and channels are required for today's Platform Marketer.

Robust scenario planning and optimization capabilities allow for forecasting across measurement levels and dimensions, and a formal testing approach allows insights to feed back into attribution. Dashboarding tools have become a critical organizational unifying tool for the Platform Marketer, offering a single place to go across the organization to gain integrated insights and reporting of customer performance.

THE TECHNOLOGY STACK

The engine that drives the efforts of the Platform Marketer is an integrated marketing technology stack that brings together first- and third-party consumer profiles and segments into the analytic and execution capabilities of highly specialized automation tools. The effective marketing technology stack facilitates easy integration and access to valuable data from numerous, disparate online and offline (CRM) data sources to give a consolidated consumer view (Figure 3.2).

This consolidated consumer view is activated and managed through the marketing database, identity management, analytics, data management platforms (DMP), decision management, and media- and channel-specific execution platforms. The open and flexible design and implementation of the stack allows for agile adaptation to the rapidly changing "data currencies" required to execute in the ever-evolving digital audience platform marketplace.

In recent months, we have seen the most advanced marketers rationalizing the marketing technology stack. This will become the focus of most marketers in the coming year. The tech stack should be able to support the major functions described in the following section.

Enabling the Competencies of the Platform Marketer

1. *Identity management, data onboarding, and tagging.* The key to unlocking your online and offline data is to identify consumers, where possible, and to understand the uniqueness of anonymous individuals. Identity management allows for the development of the "gold copy" of the online-offline consumer record. It will create a single key

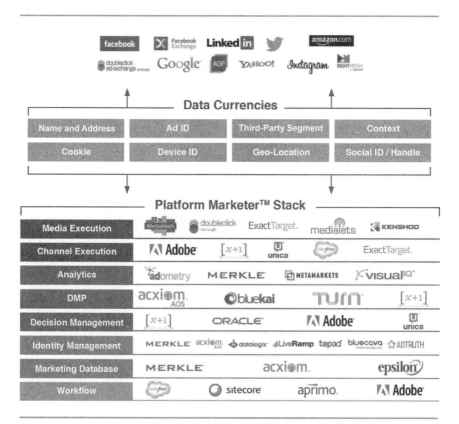

FIGURE 3.2   Enabling the Platform Marketer Competencies

that unifies personas across channels and media. It will facilitate the onboarding of offline data to enable the use of this data in the online channels. And it will have the connection to third-party sources to improve the identification of individuals across channels and devices. During the association of different customer profiles, we are also able to construct a time series of events—the event stream—related to a unique individual. This understanding will unlock all the data and help improve the performance of marketing activities.

2. *Marketing database.* The marketing database is still the core data management component of the marketing technology stack. This database manages the "gold copy" of the consumer, prospect, and associated event records and houses the "consolidated customer view." The marketing database is responsible for publishing data to other marketing technology components.

3. *Analytics.* The analytics platform transforms data into actionable insights to inform relevant marketing executions and enable measurement strategies. This platform builds the consumer event stream, which is the longitudinal record of all of the online and offline interactions with an individual. The analytics platform then performs all of the core attribution, measurement, and forecasting/scenario planning functions required to inform critical marketer decisions. This is done on one consolidated platform where business rules, attribution algorithms, and predictive models are managed through a single portal.

4. *Data management platform.* The DMP enables the creation and management of audiences for marketing and syndication to first- and third-party audience platforms. The DMP allows for anonymous and known consumer data from various data sources, including the analytics platform, marketing database, and execution platforms, for the purpose of creating and managing useful audiences. This enables these audiences to be seamlessly syndicated or pushed into execution platforms to drive decisioning, including DSPs and site optimization tools.

5. *Decision management.* Decision management is focused on operationalizing data and insights in the execution of marketing activities. It will enable the real-time optimization and personalization of marketing messages across channels and media. The decision management function should be viewed in two parts. First, there should be a single engine for common decisions shared across all channels and media. In addition, there will be channel and media engines to drive specific rules and functions. The biggest driver to data and insight continuity across all marketing channels is the shared engine. This is the most commonly overlooked part of the decision management capability.

6. *Execution currencies.* The execution currencies represent the level of granularity and the actual data transfer between the marketer platforms and audience platforms to enable targeting and optimization. Currencies have to be understood and vertically integrated into the data model, analytics and attribution, and targeting on an ongoing basis.

An advanced architecture across the entire technology stack includes well-defined interfaces between components and participating platforms. These interfaces allow for the free flow of data and insights from the enterprise data services and analytical components to the technology and platforms that execute marketing activity. The proper construction of the technology stack will accommodate the capture, aggregation, and syndication of all data to any component. This will allow any component to subscribe to the holistic view of a consumer: the consumer's past experiences with the brand, the value of the consumer to the brand, and the right message to communicate to that consumer, regardless of channel and media. Furthermore, the data and insights will be able to create richer consumer experiences by powering the optimization and personalization engines.

The biggest impediment to marketing activities is a disjointed technology stack of loosely integrated point solutions for each channel and media. This decreases resource efficiency and erodes marketing performance. Just as important as the platforms and components themselves are the pathways between them. Each component that lacks a pathway to others becomes a silo that will take significant investment to overcome or integrate.

ORGANIZING FOR SUCCESS

Historically, the daunting task of creating integrated, personalized experiences for consumers as they move across media and channels has caused disillusion in most organizations. As a result, organizational structure, operating models, and process have generally been designed to optimize on product or channel, and thus resulted in disconnected customer interactions. As the capabilities of the Platform Marketer evolve within a company, so must the organization's operating model. As addressability and Platform Marketer capabilities enable integrated and coordinated individual personalized experiences at scale, the vision of true cCRM is now attainable. To achieve it, the company's organizational structure and operating model must evolve in parallel with the development of core Platform Marketer capabilities. When this transformation happens, firms can successfully achieve the vision and rewards of cCRM.

A DEEPER LOOK

The following chapters will take a deeper dive into each of the competencies, with specific examples of companies that are taking action in these key areas of proficiency. We have enlisted the help of a number of subject matter experts, who have contributed their in-depth insight into the requirements for up-skilling and the tools necessary to succeed as a Platform Marketer.

Chapter 4   Identity Management

Special Contributor: Matthew Mobley

A key technology enablement competency for the Platform Marketer, which will unlock the value that can be driven through customer strategy, marketing measurement, and individualized consumer experiences, is identity management. It is a competency that has become increasingly complex with the explosion of digital media and channels. It has also become more polarizing for marketers and privacy advocates, as marketers drive toward more personalized interactions with their customers and prospects. For the marketer striving to develop an understanding of all the signals that indicate that the same individual is interacting with the brand, the reality is that—in terms of identity management—the ability to distinguish between John Smith and John Doe is less important than understanding the unique qualities of that individual. This statement, of course, is not to diminish the value of knowing it is Doe versus Smith. Knowing this difference allows marketers to associate the valuable data contained in traditional offline CRM data stores and maximize ongoing, loyal relationships with individual customers. But in the end, identity management is about defining uniqueness and associating experiences and characteristics to this defined uniqueness.

THE ANATOMY OF IDENTITY

The composition of an identity can be placed on a continuum where one end is the anonymous state and the other end is the known state. In the anonymous state, identity is defined by cookie, device ID, or other digital identity marker. In the known state, identity is defined by name, address, or other physical identity marker. Most of the known state identity components fall into the protected category of personally identifiable information (PII). The complexity of the identity continuum lies in the fact that not all identity attributes identify an individual uniquely; identity attributes are device and platform specific; and there is not an inherent, persistent link between these identity attributes. These complexities are the reason why brands rely on third-party vendors to help construct a map of attributes, called an identity graph, in order to recognize unique individuals (see Figure 4.1).

The identity graph can be deconstructed into three main parts: terrestrial identity, device identity, and digital identity. Each of these parts encompasses a specific set of identity attributes that may or may

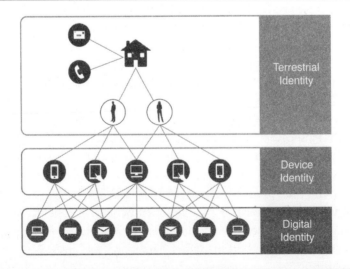

FIGURE 4.1   The Parts of the Identity Graph

not directly link to an individual but do form part of the key used to create that linkage.

TERRESTRIAL IDENTITY

The terrestrial identity is one area that marketers have, for the most part, mastered over the years. While it is not always perfect, there have been numerous platforms introduced from the 1990s to today that allow marketers to understand the association of physical identity attributes. Early on, these identity attributes consisted of name and address. They were later expanded to include attributes associated with physical addresses, for instance, phone numbers. The goal of terrestrial identity management is to maintain a persistent identifier for an individual as he moves from address to address, changes telephone numbers, and, in some cases, even changes names.

The systems that exist today parse, cleanse, associate, and manage this identifier and the associated data attributes. In some cases, they are fueled by data assets, both postal and third-party, that provide a historical view of address and name changes and their association to an array of physical identity components. These systems create the foundational identifier for the known state, where appropriate device and digital identities are associated with the terrestrial identity in order to achieve the most valuable identification of an individual. With these terrestrial, device, and digital identity associations, we can link all data assets, offline and online, to create a full profile of the individual who is interacting with the brand.

DEVICE IDENTITY

The device identity is commonly misunderstood. Often, identity attributes that relate to a device are assumed to uniquely identify an individual. While individual linkage to a device identifier can occur, it typically requires a secondary registration process, a login or consumer input form, to create this association. One of the most misunderstood is the cookie. At its core, a cookie identifies the association of a specific device and Internet browser on that device to an event. Without a secondary event, the cookie in isolation cannot be associated with an individual. Assumptions can be made but these assumptions will be complicated by the nature of the cookie.

For example, during John Doe's first visit to a site while using Internet Explorer, a cookie is placed on his laptop. John conducts a bit of research and moves on to another site. On his second visit to the site he is using Safari from his iPad. If cookies are enabled, a different cookie is placed on this device. There is no basic way to associate these cookies to each other without a third-party source or a secondary event.

There are other device identifiers. These identifiers provide for better identification of a unique device, because they are not constrained by the browser specificity issue of the cookie. At one point, the media access control (MAC) address provided a stable way to uniquely identify devices. The MAC address is a hardware-based address that provides a permanent way for companies to uniquely identify a device. In mobile devices, you also have unique device identifiers (UDID) on Apple devices and unique Android identifiers for Android devices. The use of each of these device identifiers is becoming more constrained as platform and device manufacturers become more privacy conscious. These device identifiers have been replaced on some mobile device operating systems. Apple's iOS now uses the Identifier for Advertisers (IDFA) and Google's Android now uses Google's Advertising ID (AdID). These new identifiers allow consumers more control. Consumers are able to adjust marketing preferences and change the identifier to a different value.

DETERMINISTIC VERSUS PROBABILISTIC IDENTIFICATION

As device identifiers have become more constrained in their usage, and with this trend continuing, device identification has begun to branch into a world of probabilistic identification. This world does not use deterministic methods, where the same device identifier associated with two different events is assumed to be the same device. Instead, an algorithm is applied to determine the *likelihood* that it is the same device. In recent history this has been called device fingerprinting. The market has begun to move away from this term, because it implies a more specific type of identification than is actually occurring. This is due in large part to the linguistic association to actual fingerprinting. In essence, consumers associate this with "big brother" concepts. In reality, device fingerprinting would never be as accurate as fingerprinting.

The way probabilistic matching works is that a set of data points are captured from a device. These data points would be related to certain device settings. In most cases this does not include Internet usage history. An algorithm is executed to determine the uniqueness of these settings related to all other device settings that have been captured, and a confidence score is generated that indicates the likelihood that these settings match a previously seen group of device settings. The more unique the settings, and the greater their match to previously seen settings, the more accurate the identification of a previously used device will be. Probabilistic matching breaks down as device setting uniqueness declines.

If you were to go to the store and purchase 20 new iPhones, open them, and connect them to the Internet without making any changes, there would be no way to identify each device through probabilistic matching. All the settings would be the same. If you gave these devices to 20 different people, over time, the characteristics of each phone would become more unique. The phones would be set to reflect the ways that individuals would want their devices to interact among themselves and with other devices. In time, as uniqueness increases, device identification confidence also increases.

While probabilistic identification is still considered a nascent capability, it is rapidly maturing. There are many consumer, corporate, and governmental factors that could prevent it from ever reaching its potential, but when we consider identity we need to consider both deterministic and probabilistic mechanisms.

DIGITAL IDENTITY

The digital identity constitutes the set of identity attributes that define the persona created by each individual to engage the digital world. These personas would encompass identities like Facebook user IDs, Twitter handles, forum avatars, or even login identities. The persona may or may not directly tie to an individual's physical identity attribute, but it will have a closer association to a specific individual than many device identity attributes. What makes digital identities different is that, while they may change from platform to platform, they are common across devices. A consumer's Twitter handle is the same regardless whether she is using the website or the mobile app.

Another important aspect of the digital identity is that consumers can and will associate other identity components with it. Let's look at Google+. If you create a Google+ account, you are required to provide an email address and a name. This name may or may not be your real name, but it is important as an attribute to find uniqueness in an identity graph. You may also associate your mobile number for security and for recovery of login credentials. Identity attributes collected for these purposes are typically precluded for use in marketing, but that doesn't necessarily mean they cannot be used for identification purposes. You may also associate your home-town or physical address with your Google+ account. As you can see, these digital identities can become keys to unlocking significant parts of a person's identity graph.

Not all digital identities provide the richness of the Google+ example, but they play an important role in understanding with whom we are speaking. Even in their simplest form, we will typically have an email address associated with the personal identifier (i.e., username) that is linked to a device identifier. We can begin to use these digital identities to traverse an individual's device identities, especially in the case of social media platforms where consumers have high engagement rates on multiple devices.

THE IMPACT OF THE AUDIENCE PLATFORMS ON IDENTITY MANAGEMENT

Audience platforms are digitally based, highly valued consumer services that have developed a large community of registered consumers. Registered consumers range from individuals who have created a digital identity on the platform to consumers that fully transact with the platform to receive goods or services. The best examples of these platforms are Facebook, Twitter, Google, Microsoft, Amazon, and eBay. Another key point of these platforms is that users tend to interact with them through more than one channel (e.g. mobile and website). The end result is that the platforms maintain a significant audience with which marketers can interact across channels.

Google provides a multitude of services for consumers. Its audience platform encompasses a number of services beyond just a search engine, such as social media (Google+), location services (Google Maps), and a device operating system (Android). These services can be accessed through—and will be leveraged by—a wide variety of devices and other services. The information provided by these services to consumers is greatly enhanced when consumers leverage a common login, or digital identity, across all of them. For example, search results can be tailored to your Google+ activity and location. The common login allows Google to uniquely identify that individual regardless of how the user chooses to consume these services: website, mobile app, or integrated into another service. In addition, as a consumer uses these services, Google will associate other identity attributes with this digital identity. The other attributes will entail both device and terrestrial identity components. These additional components will then allow Google to interact with the consumer, even if the person has not directly logged into the platform to access a service. In this example, Google is able to create a common map of the individual's identity attributes associated with a unique digital identity. Google then can provide access to this map in order to allow marketers to target consumers, both in the platform and in the wild.

Many of the audience platforms have extended their platforms well beyond their services. This extension is usually in the form a digital advertising network. With Facebook's acquisition of Atlas, you can now target individuals through Facebook on the broader Internet. If you want to target people who have signed up for newsletters on your company's site, you can pass those emails to Facebook to find those people in both Facebook's captive platform and in the wild, wherever Atlas reaches.

In the end, the audience platforms also have a negative impact on our ability to understand uniqueness of identities across the entirety of the digital landscape. As they encapsulate their advertising platforms for their own audiences, they are also breaking our ability to link their audience to audiences in other platforms. In essence, they are creating walled gardens (Figure 4.2). Within the confines of their platform you can achieve an understanding of the consumer and the multitude of devices they may use by leveraging the platform's unique identifier, but these identifiers do not provide a linkage to relationships in other audiences maintained by other platforms.

FIGURE 4.2   Advertising Technology Walled Gardens

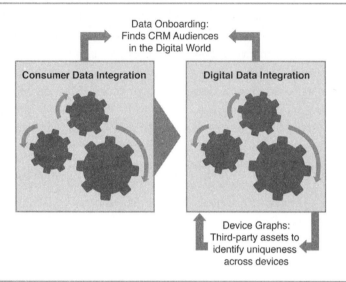

FIGURE 4.3 The Identity Engine

THE IDENTITY MANAGEMENT ENGINE

Key to identity management is having the right engine to process and manage the relationships. We won't go into detail about the engine in this chapter, but we will point out some of its most critical capabilities.

The engine provides a centralized mechanism to rationalize the terrestrial, device, and digital identity (Figure 4.3). It maintains the identities over time and is constantly revaluating the relationship of the identities to determine if new identity components create new relationships. It is an enterprise engine leveraged by the entire organization. It is informed by a stable of third-party data assets and partners, which help improve the associations that are made. These data assets and partners will be key to creating connections that your data would not be able to create in isolation, and this key will unlock your ability to activate all your data across all channels and media.

FINDING THE KNOWN PERSON IN AN ANONYMOUS WORLD

Organizations have captured vast amounts of data in existing CRM systems, and many times this data is associated with a terrestrial identity with limited or no coverage of other identity components. This data represents some of the most valuable marketing data an organization manages in its systems. The data onboarding partner will make this data available to online channels.

Data onboarding partners build identity partnerships throughout the Internet to associate terrestrial identities with device and digital identities. These partnerships, typically with large publishers or audience platforms, allow data onboarders to associate their identifiers with the registration data captured by the publishers. For instance, when you register with a content provider by providing a name, address, and email address, these publishers will fire a tag that allows a data onboarder to create an identifier associated with that registration data. A tag is a piece of code that executes on a website to exchange data between the user, the site owner, and potentially other third parties. This process, coupled with a large publisher network, gives the data onboarder the ability to create a large reference base of data identity associations.

The data onboarder will then make this reference base available to marketers. A marketer with a large offline data asset containing customers or prospects will be able to send the file to the onboarder in order to have device and digital identifiers appended to the file. This will enable the marketer to target those individuals on the Internet. One of the most common use cases is the targeting of offline consumer assets for display media. One reality marketers must contend with is that, more often than not, the data onboarder will be able to find fewer than 50 percent of your customers online. Typically, the high end of the match rate is just below 60 percent and the low end of the match rate is around 30 percent.

The overall process has many consumer privacy implications, and it is mainly regulated today by industry regulatory bodies like the Network Advertising Initiative, and each organization's consumer privacy policies. The onboarders have also established processes in order to protect consumer privacy. These processes range from not sharing the reference data directly with marketers to requiring organizations to prevent the identification of consumers without consent.

The data onboarder plays a critical role in identification. Without the data onboarders, marketers would not be able to create a large enough device and digital identity footprint within their existing CRM data assets, thus rendering one of the marketer's most valuable data assets useless in the digital world.

SEEING UNIQUENESS ACROSS MULTIPLE DEVICES

Close companions to the data onboarders are the companies that enable marketers to understand the relationship of specific device identifiers to each other. So close is the companionship that many onboarders are pushing into the cross-device identification space.

The role of the cross-device identification partner is to help marketers understand the relationship of multiple device identifiers to a single individual. In many cases, these organizations deploy probabilistic matching techniques to create these associations. They work in a similar way to the data onboarder, but they are focused on a different portion of the identity problem. For the most part, they create a reference asset that enables marketers to understand that a mobile phone, tablet, and laptop all relate to a single individual. Many of these companies do not enable you to actually identify the individual; they only allow you to know there is a relationship between device identifiers.

This portion of the identity space is still maturing, and many companies are rapidly innovating. There are organizations today that have begun to release products into the marketplace that apply probabilistic techniques in order to better associate device identities at a household level. In these newer use cases, when examining a pool of device identifiers, a marketer would be able to understand that a tablet, mobile phone, and laptop are related to an individual. The marketer would, in turn, be able to associate those devices to another individual's set of devices, potentially linking this overall group of devices to a single household.

The importance of the cross-device players extends beyond the base value of understanding device associations. The knowledge they bring to the table provides a significant marketing efficiency play. Marketers are able to better govern communication frequencies across devices. In prior instances, marketing frequency would only be managed to a single device. There are many other applications of this data, and these applications will only get better as this market matures further.

WHY UNIQUENESS IS SO IMPORTANT

Identity management is one of the most critical competencies for the Platform Marketer to understand and master. In the absence of this competency, marketers would fail to truly understand the audience or the individual with whom they are communicating. Identity management provides the map to knit together disparate data sets into a cohesive and valuable data asset for an organization. This data asset becomes the basis of an organization's customer strategy, financial measurement and reporting, and ultimately the ability of the marketer to have a meaningful, personalized experience with a consumer.

The problem with identity management is that the simplest refinement of consumer privacy regulation could have a significant impact on marketing. The fact is the vast majority of organizations are focused on leveraging their understanding of the consumer to provide the highest level of service and products. Unfortunately, there are a few bad apples that attract the attention of privacy watchdogs, threatening the efforts of legitimate marketers to provide meaningful results through identity management. We're not suggesting that marketers shouldn't be vigilant with their data oversight; we're simply pointing out that an open dialogue needs to be conducted without habitually demonizing participants.

Consider how customer relationships worked long ago. A consumer would frequent an establishment on a regular basis. Maybe this establishment was a market, restaurant, or tavern. As time progressed, the owner of the establishment would become more familiar with the patron. She would greet him as he entered the store, seat him at a good table, or even have his favorite drink ready. The owner would discuss things that were happening with her business and new products being introduced that might interest the patron. There was also an expectation by the patron. As he frequented the establishment and became more loyal, he expected the owner to recognize this loyalty and treat him accordingly. This relationship would typically never progress beyond the business. The interesting part of this example is that the ability of the business owner to build the relationship did not require her to know all of the specific identification components; she simply needed to capture enough data in her mind to know how to treat this individual as a unique person. This example is not far from the desire of marketers today. The main difference is that the data capture happens on a wider scale in a setting that is less intimate and is not well understood by the consumer. This fear of the unknown helps elevate concerns about privacy and big-brother mentality.

Marketers today need to understand uniqueness and be able to react to it. Consumers need to be educated about the value of these identity connections as well. In the absence of this understanding our world would become more and more saturated with meaningless messages from organizations trying to both retain existing customers and attract new ones. People with grown children—or no children—would see ads for diapers on every media and channel. Consumers in their early twenties would be bombarded with advertisements for reverse mortgages. Marketers need identity management to be more thoughtful and, ultimately, successful in their marketing activities.

Chapter 5 Audience Management

Special Contributor: Peter Vandre

Audience management is the discipline of identifying audiences and managing the contact strategy and corresponding conversation flow with these consumers. When done well, audience management maximizes customer value across interactive and offline touchpoints. Effective audience management is the next layer on top of a foundation of identity management. It is the role of identity management to stitch together the various unique identifiers (cookie ID, device IDs, social handles, email, address, etc.) into an identity map enabling the persistent tracking of that consumer and their actions over time. Analytics are applied to these identities to transform identities into segments that can be used to reach valuable audiences.

WHY AUDIENCE MANAGEMENT IS IMPORTANT

Publishers must manage audiences carefully to cultivate their value. Value can come in many forms, including advertiser revenue, data sales, subscription services, or product sales. If publishers maximize only the short-term value of an audience, it is often at the expense of long-term value. In the short history of the Internet, there are many instances where consumers abandoned publishers because the consumer experience was destroyed in the process of trying to monetize those audiences. Consumers have many choices, and news travels fast in cyberspace, so when they start to leave a brand, it can lead to the rapid destruction of the brand. A perfect example of this is the spectacular demise of the social network, Myspace.

As reported by *Businessweek* in June 2011, at its December 2008 peak, Myspace attracted 75.9 million unique monthly visitors in the United States, according to comScore. By May of 2014, that number had dropped to 34.8 million. Over the previous two years, Myspace had lost, on average, more than a million U.S. users a month. Because Myspace makes nearly all its money from advertising, the exodus has a direct correlation to its revenue. In 2009, the site brought in $470 million in advertising dollars, according to eMarketer. In 2011, it generated only $184 million.

What happened? Chris DeWolfe, one of the cofounders of Myspace, attributes the demise first to how they went about trying to monetize the site. "When we did the Google deal, we basically doubled the ads on our site. Remember the rotten teeth ad?" DeWolfe asks. "And the weight-loss ads that would show a stomach bulging over a pair of pants?" DeWolfe goes on to say that there was a request to stop selling these gross-out ads even if it meant a $20 million haircut on $500 million in revenue. Other decisions were made that negatively impacted revenue, for instance, the company opted not to make changes to the website that would have improved the user experience and increased page views. Things got worse for Myspace in February 2006, when Connecticut Attorney General Richard Blumenthal announced that he was launching an investigation into minors' exposure to pornography on Myspace. This created a perception that Myspace was not a safe place for kids. All of these missteps with others squandered Myspace's first mover advantage in social media as audiences fled to the greener pastures of Facebook and Twitter. Both Facebook and Twitter have found ways to monetize their audiences without ruining the customer experience and alienating users.

Audience management is just as critical for marketers as publishers. Marketers must manage consumer experience across first- and third-party audience platforms. This includes messages delivered in display ads shown on third-party sites, posts in social networks, and the user experience within the brand's first-party websites, emails, and mobile applications. And consumer expectations of marketers have never been higher. They are engaged in an ever-expanding number of channels and expect marketers to broaden their channel reach as well. They assume that brands are aware of their past interactions and expect brands to provide personalized and relevant interactions. They are self-selecting to engage with brands that provide relevance and timeliness. In July 2013, Janrain Inc. conducted a survey of 2,091 U.S. adults to uncover consumer perceptions of personalization.[1] The results showed that 74 percent of respondents get frustrated with websites when content, offers, ads, and promotions appear that have nothing to do with their interests. And 57 percent of respondents were fine with providing personal information, as long as it was for their benefit and being used in responsible ways. However, consumers desire a choice in the process. Effective audience management can mean the difference between a business crashing, like Myspace, or thriving, like Facebook and Amazon.

AUDIENCE MANAGEMENT TOOLS

There are several terms that are important to define before we dive deeper into the conversation about how to effectively manage audiences.

- *Audience* is a group of individuals (known or anonymous) who can receive a message or engage in a conversation. Online, audiences are most often associated with publishers who produce content to attract audiences. Marketers pay the publishers, either directly or indirectly, to engage with those individuals with their messages. These audiences can be accessed directly on the publishers' online properties or extended by the publishers into other third-party properties not owned by the publisher. Marketers, however, also have many first-party relationships with consumers and, as such, have audiences who visit their websites, mobile apps, social forums, and other online channels. Audience management requires publishers and marketers alike to monetize these audiences across third- and first-party properties.

---

[1] http://janrain.com/about/newsroom/press-releases/online-consumers-fed-up-with-irrelevant-content-on-favorite-websites-according-to-janrain-study/.

- *Consumer segments* are groups of individuals with similar characteristics who are assembled through an analytical process called segmentation. Segmentation enables audience management. Consumer segments can be assembled based on behavioral, attitudinal, demographic, psychographic, geographic, and other types of data. There are also many analytic methods used to create segments, ranging from simple rules to clustering to latent class models. Depending on the type of segmentation, it may be used for either strategic decisions (such as pricing or product development) or tactical decisions (such as determining the next product or message that should be shown to a person).

- *Personas* are representative members of a segment that are used to help marketers relate to that segment. For example, if we create a segment called "young new movers," we might choose Dan Smith with his family of three as the prototypical representative member of this segment based on the fact that he represents the average characteristics of individuals in this segment. Since segments are by definition mathematical formulas, they are abstract in nature and difficult for humans to digest. But personas are easily relatable, and therefore help inform the creative process.

- *Profiles* are simply statistical summaries of the elements making up a segment. Like the persona, they can help the marketer understand more about the segment. For the young mover segment, the profile could include statistics such as "75 percent of consumers in this segment are located in the United States, have an average of 1.5 children, and an average head-of-household age range between 24 and 32 years."

- *Model scores* are analytic-driven customer attributes that are used to inform targeting and personalization decisions. Whereas segmentation is used to organize individuals into groups, model scores are very granular (varying by individual level). Various analytical methods can be used to create these scores ranging from regression modeling, machine learning, and rules, to decision tree modeling.

As mentioned, segmentation is an important tool for extracting audience value. The problem is few marketers have figured out how to effectively utilize segmentation to *drive* value. It is common for an organization to rally around a major segmentation project with a promise that the output segmentation will effectively drive everything from product development to market investment to acquisition creative to real-time personalization across media and channels. A promise that a single segmentation can accomplish such a wide range of purposes is misguided and always leads to missed expectations and failed implementations—and

Dimension	Definition	Strategic				Tactical	
		Product Development	Investment Decisions	Market Analysis	Positioning and Messaging	Program Design	Individual Personalization
Attitudes and Needs	What people think	X		X	X	X	
Motivation	What motivates decision			X	X	X	
Value	Monetary value to organization		X	X			
Life Stage	Stage in life (demographic)	X					
Behavior	What people do					X	X
Life Cycle	Stage of relationship with organization	X				X	X

FIGURE 5.1   Where Different Types of Segmentation Work Best

often a devalued role and a bad reputation for segmentation within the organization.

To avoid this trap, we recommend thinking about segmentation across several dimensions. Different segment dimensions are useful for different business purposes. Figure 5.1 contains a table that summarizes common segment dimensions with their definitions and recommended applications.

As a rule of thumb, some segmentation dimensions are more suited for strategic applications and others for more tactical marketing execution. When we are informing an individual-level communication decision, strategic segmentation dimensions are often not as helpful. In these use cases, individual customer behavior and life cycle are typically the most powerful inputs. On the other hand, research-driven segmentation, rich in consumer attitudes, needs, motivations, and life stage segments, are incredibly valuable in informing strategic business decisions through the customer lens.

The best overarching segmentation strategies are multidimensional. Figure 5.2 illustrates how one financial services company segmented its customers across different dimensions to effectively inform strategic and tactical decisions.

Segmentation / Model	Description	Primary Inputs	Uses
Enterprise Segmentation	Attitudinal, behavioral, and demographic segmentation scored across prospects and customers	• Customer survey • Customer behavior • Demographic overlay	• Product development • Market analysis • Positioning and messaging • Program design
Value Segmentation	Current and predicted potential value across prospects and customers	• Account and product data • Transaction history • Credit score proxy • Share of wallet estimates	• New investment • Marketing spend allowable by customer • Customer portfolio management
Life Cycle Segmentation	Shows progression from prospect to multiproduct buyer	• Customer transaction history	• Consumer-level targeting and personalization • Program development and planning • Customer portfolio management
Audience Target Models	High-value audience flags driving targeting decisions (often real-time)	• Trigger behaviors (ex. email sign-up, abandon application, social platform engagement) • Remarketing groups • Look-alike groups	• Customer-level targeting
Next-Best Action Models	Real-time updated segments indicating next best product, message, offer, and channel to inform next step in conversation	• Digital behavior (real-time) • Contextual data (real-time) • Device data (real-time) • Online and offline transactions • Preference data • Segments (enterprise, value, life cycle)	• Customer-level targeting and personalization

FIGURE 5.2   Comprehensive Audience Management Toolset

With this audience management framework, the company is able to drive strategic direction through the enterprise segments, while taking advantage of the much more granular "audience targeting" and "next-best-action" models to drive individual-level targeting and messaging decisions. The value segmentation plays a dual role. It is used to inform macro business investment decisions but also serves as a guardrail to ensure that marketers aren't overinvesting in specific individuals. Future plans for the value dimension include pushing it into the demand-side platform to inform bid levels and contact frequency, especially when remarketing to existing customers.

One of the most important considerations in creating any segmentation or predictive model is the ability to accurately score across the audiences for which marketers intend to apply it. This may seem obvious but we've seen many instances, for example, where a pure research-based segmentation is developed with little to no thought for how that segmentation can be scored against the target audience universe.

Another consideration is how the segmentation or model can be scored against anonymous audiences. Up until a few years ago, segmentation was scored only on universes that had personally identifiable information attached. With many of today's audience platforms enabling only marketing to anonymous individuals, this is no longer an option.

Some questions you might ask your analytics team before they start a segmentation project include:

- What are the purpose and intended uses of the segmentation?
- To what specific audiences will we be able to apply this segmentation and with what level of accuracy?
- Is this a segment that can and should be scored in real time (given the desired application use cases)? What system or application will be doing this scoring?
- Can and should this segmentation be applied to first- and/or third-party anonymous segments? What data will be available to facilitate that?

WHEN SEGMENTATION DISAPPOINTS

If segmentation is so powerful, why does it sometimes fall short of expectations? There are various reasons for this:

- *The misconception that segmentation will directly create business return.* Simply creating differentiated, mutually exclusive groups, even when implemented, does not change customer behaviors. Segmentation differs from predictive modeling. Models select target audiences using a fact-based cutoff of the model scores. In other words, we are stacking the deck to make sure the marketing initiatives work and predicting who will respond or convert. Segmentation is not targeted to the individual and, in that way, it differs from predictive modeling.
- *Thinking of segmentation as a substitute for targeting.* The purpose of segmentation is not to target a specific marketing campaign, and the reason for that is simple: If we want to target something with accuracy, there is always a better way to do it than building mutually exclusive

groups, for example, through building propensity models. Targeting and personalization require real-time contextual information that is not available when creating customer segments.

- *Creating segments to purely understand a conceptual mind-set or persona.* Often, agencies and consulting companies build research-led "attitudinal" segments. Those have their purpose but are not relevant to selecting marketing actions. Pure research-led efforts are more like academic studies, but if they cannot convert into core strategic segments, then they are likely not going to bring the desired change.
- *Excessive focus on demographics.* Although demographic personas and profiles are very easily understood, they are often weakly tied to use or purchase orientation and, therefore, unconvincingly tied to monetary outcomes. Of course, the entire measurement system of U.S. television advertising still uses age as a primary cut, so we do not imply that demographics have no use. Our point is that demographics represent only one dimension of a much broader picture.
- *Undue absorption in the segmentation's technical details.* Too often, analytical efforts place too much focus on the methodology and tactics of the design and ignore the ultimate purpose and goal of the solution. This typically happens when there is no clear purpose for the segmentation solution. A well-crafted strategy yields a meaningful segmentation that is homogeneous within segments but different across segments. Although the latter pieces can be quantified, it is hard to put a metric against what is meaningful. The contrast to this is modeling, where, typically, a clear metric is optimized. So the analytic methodology, although important, can be a secondary focus.

ACTIVATING AUDIENCES

Historically, segmentation was used in digital media primarily as a rough tool for audience planning and buying. The process works as follows.

1. Marketer or agency conducts primary and secondary research to determine the target audience and its associated characteristics.
2. Agency creates basic demographic-based segments that are colored with additional research and presented through personas.
3. Mass and digital marketing agency takes personas and leverages planning tools to try and match them to specific digital properties and the broader media buy.

4. Budgets are allocated accordingly and inventory is secured for those properties.
5. Media is run and performance monitored as adjustments are made.

In this situation, segmentation is playing an important role in informing macro spend decisions, but it is still a relatively blunt instrument. However, as more and more audiences are becoming addressable through audience platforms, the role of segmentation is becoming much more important. Although it is still used at a macro level to inform those guaranteed and often premium ad placements, it is doing much more heavy lifting within programmatic media. For example, segments can be created for high-value audiences (leveraging first- and third-party data) that are then sent (syndicated) from data management platforms (DMP) to audience platforms for targeting with specific messages. Customer value metrics can be used to turn off or throttle up marketing to specific individuals. Life cycle and next-best-action segments are key inputs into the decision management platform where rules and optimization algorithms are leveraged to drive the most impactful communication delivery at each consumer touchpoint.

So, what does effective audience management look like from a customer experience standpoint? Imagine a progression of customer interactions such as depicted in Figure 5.3. Here we have paired what the customer is experiencing within a customer journey with what the Platform Marketer is doing.

This experience shows that segmentation is informing marketing actions at each step in the customer experience. For this to work, it is essential that the segmentation be regularly scored and updated, often in real time, to inform successive consumer interactions with the brand. The DMP is doing a lot of heavy lifting in regard to managing these segments in interactive channels. However, the DMP must be syncing with the foundational marketing platform to create a complete view of the customer. It also must have a tight connection to the insight platform where new segmentations are created and deployed and where performance is tracked.

TYING AUDIENCE MANAGEMENT TO MARKETING PERFORMANCE

For audience management to be effective there must be accountability and performance tracking against each segment throughout the entire

Customer Interaction	Audience Management Actions
New product is created to target an underserved segment and advertised through mass media	• Enterprise segmentation informs strategic opportunities to serve the market with a new product • This segmentation is coupled with expected lifetime value estimates to size opportunity • Decision is made to introduce a pilot program • TV planners buy TV spots against target demographics
Prospect sees ads on Facebook and other sites for product	• Initial experience with corresponding creative treatments and messaging are inspired based on target enterprise segment characteristics • Individuals are placed in high-value prospect segment based on offline and online prospect models; segments are synced with DMP for online targeting • Contact frequency is tracked against segment and capped at five contacts per week
Individual clicks through an ad and hits a landing page for product	• Landing page content is personalized based on whether the individual is a prospect; best message, product, and offer are reflected in the landing page experience • Individual is added to remarketing segment for cookie level-targeting through paid search and display • Remarking segment updates are syndicated to Google and other audience platforms for targeting in near real time, along with recommended messaging
Individual purchases product offline and is sent an email confirmation	• Life cycle segment is updated from prospect to new customer • Next best product and offer segments are updated in real time and reflected in cross-sell message through confirmation email • Customer value metrics are updated based on recent purchase along with new marketing allowable • Individual is added to new remarketing segment for new customers with loyalty message • Segment is syndicated to social audience platforms with a share-with-friend message

FIGURE 5.3 Typical Customer Experience within the Customer Journey

marketing execution process. This includes not only the purchase of media, but also the delivery of that media, and its associated impact on conversions and the creation of incremental value.

Verifying that the media was correctly purchased against the desired segment is the first step in this process. This requires analytics to be able to configure campaign tracking with the right metadata so that it is easy to report out spend by segment across tactics. Because this is a difficult task, enforcing consistent and accurate entry of metadata by media planners has been a challenge since the beginning of digital marketing.

Next, we must be able to verify that media was delivered to segments as planned. This is also very difficult and requires constant vigilance. A big part of the challenge is that there are incentives within the digital media ecosystem for publishers and data providers to cut corners or commit fraud to increase revenue. Examples of this are the high levels of ad fraud we see among unscrupulous publishers who will use bots to boost impression and click delivery numbers. *Adweek* reported in October 2013 that one in every six PCs may be infected with bots.[2] Fraudsters are posing under the names of legitimate publishers, making it difficult for the marketer to distinguish high-quality from low-quality delivery. Third-party data providers also have incentives to bend the rules and supply intender or other audiences, using loose definitions of intender to boost audience sizes at the expense of quality. And, unfortunately, marketing agencies are also sometimes not incented to do the right thing. An agency that finds that its target click rate is below goal for a month may turn a blind eye or even increase spend to a suspicious publisher that is providing click rates. The Platform Marketer is an audience management expert who stays on top of these issues.

Finally, as mentioned in Chapter 11, Measurement and Attribution, the ability to report out marketing performance by segment is essential to a segment-driven marketing strategy. Attribution reports, dashboards, and planning tools should be filterable by key segments.

CONCLUSION

Just as audience management builds on the Platform Marketer competency of identity management, other competencies can only be done well

---

[2] www.adweek.com/news/advertising-branding/online-ad-fraudsters-are-stealing-6-billion-brands-152823.

on a solid foundation of audience management. The segmentation and model underpinning of audience management is the scaffolding that supports the customer journey strategy, which cuts across digital media and channel optimization. It is one of the primary lenses through which attribution and planning must occur. And it is only possible through thoughtful integration across each component of the technology stack.

Chapter 6   The Privacy Paradox

Special Contributor: Bennie Smith

The Platform Marketer wants nothing more than to meet consumer expectations by delivering a rich, personalized experience across the devices they love and constantly use. The Platform Marketer dedicates significant resources toward making that a reality. And while consumers intuitively know that those experiences are informed by information, they are often reluctant to provide it. They are often uneasy with the idea that marketers may have access to information about them to which they don't have visibility themselves. This reflects the commonly held definition of privacy as "the right to be let alone," and it speaks to consumers' desire to be in control of how, when, and with whom they interact. To add to the challenge, marketers don't always know how to ask for the data or how to use it in ways that meet the needs and expectations of the consumer.

For the Platform Marketer, therein lies the opportunity. It's the Platform Marketer who can chart the course that results in respectfully reaching the consumer; delivering value into the customer relationship, regardless of channel, device, or platform; incorporating a full understanding of the challenges and sensitivities of each touchpoint; and remaining in full alignment with both consumer preferences and corporate objectives.

CONSUMER CONCERNS

In order to find solutions that address consumers' concerns around privacy, it's important to listen to what they are saying. Typical research in this area tends to generalize rather than break down concerns by categories of interaction or experience. While the research around consumer privacy is varied and, in some cases, gives off conflicting or unclear messages, there is a signal among the noise.

In the GFK Survey on Data Privacy and Trust, conducted in March 2014,[1] 59 percent of respondents, who spanned all age groups, expressed growing concern over privacy in the previous 12 months (see Figure 6.1). Given the increasing frequency of blaring headlines about data breaches at large and small businesses, retailers, and restaurants—coupled with the general unease around the notion of pervasive government surveillance—it is no wonder that concern over personal data is high.

This is not the first time we've seen high sensitivity or concerned responses from consumers on this issue, but maybe it's the first time we've seen them in conjunction with consumer action in response.

In "The Data Digest: The Evolution of Consumer Attitudes on Privacy," published August 1, 2014, by Forrester,[2] we see that consumer behavior can change in response to concerns they feel overall about privacy (Figure 6.2).

Despite the lack of granularity in a lot of the research, there are some clear messages that can map out a path to opportunity for the Platform Marketer to carve out a different experience for consumers.

This is supported by the GFK Data Privacy and Trust study that shows consumers, while looking for more order and clarity regarding their data in the online space, are not calling for governments to step in and fix the problem through regulatory or legislative efforts—at least not yet. Instead,

---

[1] GFK Survey on Data Privacy and Trust, "Data Highlights," March 2014, www.gfk.com/trustsurvey/Pages/default.aspx.
[2] http://blogs.forrester.com/anjali_lai/14-08-01-the_data_digest_the_evolution_of_consumer_attitudes_on_privacy?evar1=51174:1444729&cmpid=PR:soc:tw:Shout+1444729.

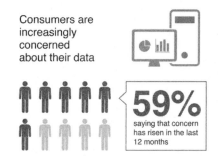

Consumers are increasingly concerned about their data

59% saying that concern has risen in the last 12 months

FIGURE 6.1   Growing Consumer Concern about Their Data
Source: GFK Survey on Data Privacy and Trust—Data Highlights, 2014, www.gfk.com/trustsurvey/Pages/default.aspx.

Consumers feel more empowered about their privacy than they did a year ago

● Community members who have taken steps to protect their personal data

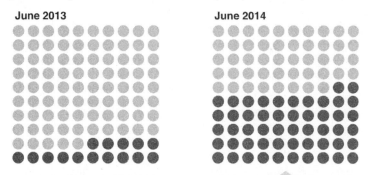

June 2013

June 2014

Top three steps that consumers have taken in order to protect their personal data:
1. Changed privacy settings on my social networking account
2. Installed privacy protection tools (e.g., Adblock)
3. Changed my mobile phone provider

FIGURE 6.2   Growing Consumer Empowerment
Base: 600 U.S. online adults.
Source: Forrester's ConsumerVoices Market Research Online Community, Q3 2013 (U.S.) and Forrester's ConsumerVoices Market Research Online Community, Q2 2014 (U.S.).

FIGURE 6.3   Consumer Desire for Better Data Controls

they want the change to come from those brands with which they already interact and that have their data in their care, custody, or control.

It's no wonder consumers feel this way; these are the places and communities with which they spend increasing amounts of time and disclose all kinds of personal, if not sensitive, information (Figure 6.3).

If those brands don't take this opportunity to better engage on the issues that are of concern to the consumer, those consumers will take action by using the tools at their disposal to gain whatever measure of control they can. The marketers who look for and listen to the signal within the noise will ultimately prevail in providing their consumers with those rich, tailored, personalized experiences that lead to long-term, high-value customer relationships.

THE "PRIVACYSCAPE"

Some marketers may dismiss or minimize consumer feedback and behaviors as the anxieties of a few or believe that their already established customer relationships don't require much additional reflection on their part. But the Platform Marketer knows the folly of this thinking and is also keenly aware that it's not just the consumer who has concerns about privacy.

Some years ago, Terence Kawaja, CEO of LUMA Partners, developed the LUMAscape to clarify marketers' thinking about the digital marketing landscape and all of the entities sitting between them and the consumer. Along those lines, we created a landscape, or "privacyscape," for the Platform Marketer (see Figure 6.4). It illustrates that the space between

FIGURE 6.4   Privacyscape

the Platform Marketer and the consumer is filled with multiple groups of stakeholders—from industry self-regulatory to state-mandated regulatory to legislative—all of which have a voice in the consumer privacy conversation.

While this is not an exhaustive list of all the entities across the globe that have a stake in shaping consumer privacy, it does illustrate that the path from marketer to consumer is one that has to be navigated carefully and respectfully. This is particularly true when we look at some of the public statements made by regulators and privacy advocates. "It's safe to promise you that 2014 will be just as busy as 2013," said Jessica Rich, director, FTC Bureau of Consumer Protection, speaking at an International Association of Privacy Professionals meeting in December 2013.[3] And while speaking at the National Advertising Division Annual Conference on September 30, 2013, she said, "We've spent a lot of time thinking not just about what is being marketed to consumers but also how items are marketed, especially in the mobile arena."[4]

---

[3] www.ftc.gov/sites/default/files/documents/public_statements/privacy-today-ftcs-2014-privacy-agency/131206privacytodayjrich.pdf.
[4] www.ftc.gov/sites/default/files/documents/public_statements/remarks-national-advertising-division-annual-conference/130930nad.pdf.

FIGURE 6.5   Attention and Enforcement
Source: DataGuidance, *Enforcement Report 2013.* © 2014, Cecile Park
Publishing, Ltd., London, www.ftc.gov/enforcement/cases-proceedings.

It's not just empty rhetoric; attention like this has led to greater scrutiny and, in many cases, action, as depicted in Figure 6.5, has taken the form of press attention as well regulatory enforcement both in the United States and in the European Union.

Let's take a look at three of the main stakeholders in the protection of consumer privacy.

GOVERNMENT

Governments tend to legislate in a rearview mirror sort of fashion. In other words, they often try to prevent something that has already happened from happening again in the future. Even if a mishap is imminent, legislative intervention is often too late to be truly proactive in avoiding unwanted situations. In the United States, the laws intending to protect consumer privacy in some way can be focused on specific industries, like financial services (Gramm–Leach–Bliley Act, 1999); or healthcare (Health Insurance Portability and Accountability Act of 1996); channels of communication, like email (CAN-SPAM Act of 2003); or protected classes of people, namely children, as we saw in the Children's Online Privacy Protection Act of 1998. The European Union adopted the Data Protection Directive in 1995 that speaks to the protection of individuals with respect to the processing of personal data and the movement of that data. In 2015, the existing directive, it is believed, will be superseded by the General Data Protection Regulation. In both cases, the law is broad and comprehensive and rests on the idea that an individual's privacy is a basic human right.

In addition to legislation, governments can promote concepts of consumer privacy by imbuing regulatory agencies with the authority to either enforce existing laws or create regulations and standards that can act in the absence of legislation. In the United States, the Federal Trade Commission (FTC) is perhaps the best example of this. At the top of the commission's list of strategic goals is the protection of consumers against fraud, deception, and unfair practices in the marketplace. On issues of consumer privacy, the FTC has been a supporter, and at times a not-so-gentle reminder, of the importance of vigorous and responsive industry self-regulation.

While there are differing opinions as to the efficacy of legislation and/or regulatory policy, this approach can often provide at least some clarity to the Platform Marketer as to where the boundary lines are in terms of behavior and practices. This stability can help the Platform Marketer plan and develop customer engagement models that speak to corporate objectives and consumer expectations, while living squarely within the regulatory requirements. The Platform Marketer might say that CAN-SPAM is an example of this. While it's not perfect, and there continue to be areas of debate and ambiguity, there is enough clarity that over the decade since it was enacted, we have been able to develop strong, robust, and effective consumer messaging campaigns that have acquired and retained customers in a rich value-driven relationship.

The Platform Marketer also recognizes that it is important to be aware of any regulatory issues that are being addressed at the state level. We know that achieving federal legislation is often difficult and can take years to accomplish; however, state legislators tend to move somewhat more quickly in their attempt to fill a void created by federal inaction, particularly when it comes to the perceived well-being of citizens. California is just one example of a state that has taken this responsibility seriously. Over the years, the state has enacted privacy legislation that not only includes a fair number of general privacy laws but also specific ones that focus on health information, identity theft, unsolicited commercial communications, and online privacy. These protections are all rooted in the California Constitution, Article 1, Section 1, giving each citizen an "inalienable right" to pursue and obtain "privacy," a very worthy objective.[5]

INDUSTRY

Once issues of concern have been identified and solutions are proposed, it's not always true that legislation, either at the national or state level, is the best answer to address the problem. Often, it is the industry itself, in the form of self-regulatory organizations, that can step up and provide the necessary protections for consumers. These measures come in the form of widely accepted best practices or guidelines. The Network Advertising Initiative (NAI) is an example of an industry coming together and formulating a code of conduct that is broadly adopted by members in the online advertising space. For the most part, NAI is favorably viewed by regulators as a strong and acceptable alternative to legislations. The Platform Marketer knows that this approach is substantive and meaningful, yet flexible enough to be adaptive to the changing nature of the environments in which consumers congregate. Self-regulation is also responsive to the dynamic and innovative technologies that power these market fluctuations.

It is in the adherence to and promotion of industry self-regulatory practices based on the FTC's Fair Information Practice Principles that the idea of protecting the consumer from deceptive or unfair practices can come to life, creating a distinction between those who value the consumer and those who have other goals. The Platform Marketer understands that the basic principles of notice and choice, as outlined in the brand's Fair Information Practices Policy, are the building blocks of the foundation upon which the consumer relationship is built.

INDIVIDUALS

Often overlooked, but just as important a stakeholder, is the consumer who plays a large role in the notion of the privacy paradox. Consumer engagement levels in all manner of digital experiences and communities

---

[5] www.leginfo.ca.gov/.const/.article_1.

have simply exploded—and they show little or no signs of slowing. There is an awareness among consumers, not only that their personal data helps to drive the rich experiences that these companies provide, but also that sharing this data is the price you pay for these experiences, in whole or in part. Without a better understanding of the what, when, and why of data collection and use, the consumer is often left feeling vulnerable and conflicted. "I love this restaurant-finder app on my phone, but what happens to my data if I press 'ok' when asked if that app can use my current location?" Armed with tools that can provide them options, the consumer moves from passive bystander to active participant.

Through the adoption of privacy-protecting tools and practices, such as downloading and keeping updated versions of antivirus programs, running the latest versions of software on devices, utilizing browser controls to limit some or all cookies, and even installing ad blockers, consumers are demonstrating their ability to control the environments in which they congregate and reveal themselves. Another indicator is this Google Trends reporting (see Figure 6.6) showing the number of consumer searches for the term "ad block" substantially increasing over time.

Again, the Platform Marketer can look at this challenge and see an opportunity that lies in searching out ways to provide consumers with the

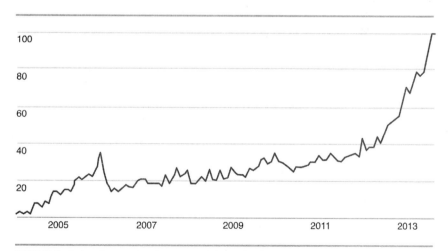

FIGURE 6.6   Consumer Interest in Ad Blocking
Source: http://invenio-solutions.com/online-consumer-privacyhow-will-it-affect-the-media-brands-you-love/.

experiences they are looking for, along with an understanding of how their personal data supports them.

The Platform Marketer and team are aware of the debate emerging around the need to update or revisit some basic principles that shape the ways we've typically approached privacy. A number of privacy approaches exist around the globe that vary by jurisdiction. For example, in the United States there is a sectoral approach to privacy protections at the regulatory level while the EU has adopted a broad-based, comprehensive approach to the problem. Both, however, have roots in the Fair Information Practice Principles, which date back to the early 1970s. These guidelines were developed in response to the issue of an increased use of automated data systems that contained information about individuals.[6]

Notice and choice are at the heart of those principles and have been effective in communicating to consumers the information needed to make decisions about how to engage with brands in the online space. However, this becomes more complicated as the traditional distinctions between the first- and third-party roles, responsibilities, and data ownership become cloudier. This is particularly true as it concerns collection and usage of data. A more robust model is needed to communicate important information to consumers. The Platform Marketer is spending time with the team, thinking through ways to do just that and realizing that it's not only notice, but transparency, that consumers need (see Figure 6.7). It's no longer just a "tell them" approach but rather "show them" via more means of communication than simply text-dependent disclosures. Additionally, the Platform Marketer and team know that simple, binary choice options like yes or no, subscribe or unsubscribe—and the all-or-nothing approach they dictate—are not likely the best way to capture consumer engagement. Instead, providing consumers with a greater sense of control over the data is a better approach for the long term. How do notice and choice work when my watch is collecting data about me, my movements, and my behaviors in order to help me make more health-conscious choices that can lead to better physical and emotional outcomes?

---

[6] U.S. Secretary's Advisory Committee on Automated Personal Data Systems, Records, Computers and the Rights of Citizens, "Chapter IV: Recommended Safeguards for Administrative Personal Data Systems" (1973).

Notice	versus	Transparency
Tell them		Show them
Fixed / non-dynamic		Omni-present
Text only / text heavy		Text + image + video

Choice	versus	Control
Binary "opt-in / opt-out"		Buffet / à la carte
Based on interest of the first party		User experience or circumstance driven
Text only / text heavy		Customized

FIGURE 6.7   Notice to Transparency and Choice to Control

THE PLATFORMS

In addition to understanding the regulatory framework at the national, state, and industry level, the Platform Marketer must also develop a solid understanding of the use requirements of the key platforms on which consumers are being engaged. Typically, that includes Google, Facebook, and Twitter, and, depending on your social media strategy and understanding of consumers' habits, it may extend to YouTube, Pinterest, Yahoo!, AOL, and others.

For the most part, the common thread running through their policy statements speaks to the advertisers' responsibility for the safety and legitimacy of their ads and/or messages. That's no surprise for the Platform Marketer, as these principles apply in the offline world as well. What may be different for the Platform Marketer is the application of these principles in the online space, particularly when engaging consumers in a social media setting. With the proliferation of "liking," "poking," "friending," and "following"—not to mention sharing content and promotions—it's important for the Platform Marketer and team to develop internal best-practice guidelines about how and when to participate and engage.

These guidelines may be platform specific, such as Twitter, and center around the unique aspects of that community. They should address questions that include: What are the criteria for when your brand follows an individual? Should you proactively seek to do that or wait for an invitation from the consumer? How do you handle negative tweets? Is there a tiger team in place to address questions or misinformation? Do you have multilanguage skills on the team? (You may be targeting English-speaking consumers in the United States, but your tweets may not be limited to an English-speaking audience, especially if they are widely shared or retweeted.) Are corporate PR and marketing communications looped into the strategy in case your organization becomes part of "the story" that gains broad or mainstream media attention?

Additionally, a set of internal best-practice guidelines are extra important for the Platform Marketer whose organization sits within an industry that is more explicitly regulated than others. Pharma and financial services are just two examples of industries whose marketing and advertising practices and activities may be subject to law at the national and local levels, governed by industry self-regulatory codes of conduct as well as specific requirements and/or prohibitions imposed by the platforms themselves.

It is typical for financial services marketers to ensure that their messages and promotions are compatible with the disclosure requirements imposed by law or industry code of conduct when they appear in traditional channels like print or television. However, it's the Platform Marketer who must ensure that the requirements originating from the platforms themselves are equally addressed when messages appear in online spaces as display ads or search queries, or in social media spaces, as tweets, for example. Twitter, like the other platforms, explicitly calls out its expectation of the Platform Marketer to act in compliance with these standards.

In some cases, there are broad restrictions of use, either by country or by product or service being promoted, and prior approval may be required. In the case of health and pharma marketing, the Platform Marketer understands that the requirements around promoting over-the-counter medications in a medium with limited real estate for disclosure makes product description a challenge but not necessarily impossible.

In the same way the Platform Marketer sees the ongoing need to communicate to the customer, so do the platforms themselves. One example of this is the continual efforts of Facebook to find ways to better communicate with its users the ways in which it collects and uses data that powers the experience now and in the future.

Facebook has taken steps to make the information clear and accessible, utilizing an interactive, colorful site with language designed to be easier to understand and absorb. "This is a continued effort," said Facebook Chief Privacy Officer Erin Egan, recognizing the frustration that users may

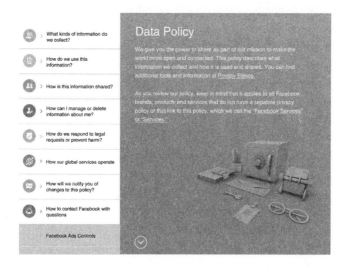

FIGURE 6.8   Facebook Data Policy

experience due to the scope and/or frequency of change to their privacy settings (Figure 6.8). "We want to provide information to people in a clear and concise manner."[7]

As the Platform Marketer begins to utilize multiple platforms as part of the customer acquisition and/or customer retention efforts, it will become increasingly important to note that these underlying policies and guidelines are subject to change. This is especially true if that platform continually rolls out new services, products, and tools or updates existing ones that may impact how data is collected and/or used. As those changes may subsequently impact how the Platform Marketer interacts with the platform directly or with consumers present on the platform. They all require the Platform Marketer to take the responsibility of compliance with their changing guidelines and rules. The savvy marketer directs the team to come up with solutions that address this responsibility. These tactics could include a process such as setting up a recurring calendar event that triggers the designated team member(s) to revisit the policies and guidelines of the respective platforms to see if the last updated date remains the same as previously noted. If the date has changed, organize

---

[7] www.washingtonpost.com/blogs/the-switch/wp/2014/11/13/facebook-rewrites-its-privacy-policy-so-that-humans-can-understand-it.

the team for a discussion around whether those changes impact the strategy or any of the previously or soon-to-be deployed tactics.

At this point, it may not be clear to the average marketer how to find the opportunity in what is developing into an increasingly challenging environment, full of cautious consumers and ever-watchful advocates and regulators. The Platform Marketer, on the other hand, recognizes that there are two key assets that can help to level the playing field and create opportunity where it may not seem to exist.

The first and foundational asset is the customer relationship. It is often overlooked or undervalued as a core principal, but the Platform Marketer is the only stakeholder who owns the other half of the customer relationship. This is a powerful asset through which to both communicate with and listen to the consumer.

Think about this as an example: After years of shopping in the bricks and mortar locations of a major national retailer, a consumer decides to explore shopping and buying online with that retailer by agreeing to opt in to its email messaging program. It all seems very simple and straightforward. Almost immediately after receiving the welcome message, the consumer begins to see information and offers about the upcoming season's fashions or back-to-school specials. After several days, the retailer sends a promotional message that also contains the opportunity to customize the content of future messaging according to the consumer's self-reported gender-based preferences. The preference information is entered, the form submitted, and the consumer receives an email confirmation of receipt. A day later, the next email communication arrives in the consumer's inbox, but it does not reflect the self-reported preferences of the consumer. Assuming some sort of mistake, the consumer finds the customer service email address in the message and sends an email asking why, after taking the time to communicate her preferences, she is still receiving offers that are irrelevant to those preferences. The marketer acknowledges the receipt of the inquiry and sets expectations about a response timeline (good) and a personalized response arrives within 24 hours (good). However, the answer as to why the consumer is still getting irrelevant messaging is that it takes three to four weeks for the retailer's systems to be fully updated with the new information. That is a poor response and an even worse experience for the consumer.

What the Platform Marketer knows is that, when we ask consumers to provide information about what they value in the relationship—which is what self-reported preferences are—it is essential to incorporate that into the customer relationship in ways that acknowledge the consumer.

If there are real technical limitations that cannot be overcome in the short term, the Platform Marketer knows that the answer is not to continue delivering irrelevant (unwanted) information to the consumer until back-end or legacy systems have been populated with the new data. Instead you must look for alternatives to a negative consumer experience. One option might be to temporarily suppress that user altogether to ensure she doesn't receive additional irrelevant messages during the time it takes to put the technical capabilities in place. Another option might be to proactively craft temporary messaging that informs the customer of the time it will take to incorporate her self-reported data, with an assurance that her preferences will be incorporated into the brand's communications as quickly as possible. This approach allows the marketer to maintain engagement with that consumer, but does not imply that her expressed preferences are being ignored because of technical limitations. The Platform Marketer seeks to avoid experiences that subtly or otherwise communicate to the customer that her feedback or input is not valued.

While this one issue may seem like a small thing, given the amount of inbound mail the average inbox receives—up to 81 individual messages each day in 2014 (see Figure 6.9)—the Platform Marketer knows how critical it is for messaging to stand out in the consumer's inbox. That goal can't be achieved by ignoring customer signals. Doing so could relegate all future messaging to the status of spam, which is defined by the recipient as messaging that is not meaningful or relevant to her, regardless of whether it was solicited. The Platform Marketer is looking for ways to incorporate

Average Number of Emails Received	2013	2014	2015
Total	78	81	84
Legitimate Email	65	68	71
Spam	13	13	13

FIGURE 6.9   Email versus Spam
Source: "E-Mail Statistics Report 2011–2015," The Radicati Group.

those responses and to take action on them in ways that drive value and create a sense of trust.

The other critical asset the Platform Marketer has is the team—the set of internal resources including privacy, legal, and data security—that can be marshaled and used to effectively establish a strong, value-based, two-way communication with the consumer. While everyone on the team has a role to play, all the activities are organized around a single guiding principle: how our brand delivers upon the promise of rich, personalized experiences while respecting the expectations of the customer.

Thinking back a moment to the findings in the GFK Survey on Data Privacy and Trust, we know that consumers are suspicious of many organizations that have custody of their data. They worry that their personal information is not being handled in ways that ensure its protection from breaches, malicious threats, or unexpected use. That's where your data security team steps in. Are they providing you with a quarterly assessment of both what's happening externally and how that may be shaping your organization's global information security program—particularly as it regards the security of customer data? The challenge for the Platform Marketer and the data security resources is to provide the transparency required to increase customer confidence but at the same time to avoid providing a roadmap to those who would misuse the data. The answer may be different by industry or for each individual organization; one place to start would be the privacy policy. Is there a section titled "data security" that can be easily found by the consumer? What level of assurance does it provide beyond the now standard "we take data security seriously" disclosure? Today's consumers are savvy enough to know that a serious approach to data security is table stakes, and they have come to expect more. Recently, a national retailer experienced an attack that resulted in the loss of millions of customer records, blaring negative headlines, and ultimately a change in leadership. A review of that privacy policy after the breach revealed that the company dedicated a mere 150 words out of almost 3,000 to describe its commitment to this increasingly important issue. While it could be argued that this company used other channels like direct mail or email to talk about these issues with both affected and unaffected consumers, the fact remains that the privacy policy is a platform that should be thought of as part of the messaging opportunity.

The third component of the team is the privacy/data protection resource, or chief privacy officer (CPO), who is the information privacy professional in the organization. In some organizations this resource is part of the legal team and perhaps the two roles are combined into the same person. However, the organizational structure does not diminish the Platform Marketer's reliance on this key resource. The CPO helps to shape and inform the organization's information collection, sharing and use practices, and the policies (if not contractual requirements) that support the principles of notice and choice.

The Platform Marketer requires the team member responsible for privacy to stay current on both global and local enforcement trends and legislative and/or regulatory initiatives that may present risk to established policies and procedures. The CPO must develop risk management strategies for new or existing products or services (privacy by design), guide training and awareness programs (e.g., Cookies and Pixels in Digital Marketing 101), and perhaps most of all, provide thought leadership on these key issues so that the Platform Marketer and team can achieve the original objective of delivering rich, tailored, and personalized experiences to the consumer in ways that meet or exceed expectations, while respecting privacy.

When the Platform Marketer and the team—especially the CPO— establish a close and mutually supportive dialogue, the Platform Marketer can come to rely on this resource as the voice of the consumer, providing insight and guidance around the thinking and actions of privacy advocates and regulators and combine that into a narrative that highlights key or emerging themes in the consumer privacy space.

An important example would be the transformation of the now basic "notice and choice" concepts into "transparency and control." It is the CPO who can help the Platform Marketer set and execute against strategy to collect, use, and share consumer data. It used to be enough to assume that consumers were aware when marketers were collecting data—"enter your email address here"—for example. However, with an exploding number of nontraditional sources of data that can be used to enrich the brand's understanding of the consumer and how to serve her, it places a greater obligation on the Platform Marketer to discover better, more robust ways to present and share this information. Perhaps a less obvious example of the importance of this transition can be found when we look to our friends in the European Union. In the EU, data protection authorities have long said that providing individuals with control over their data was a critical priority, particularly where practices were thought to be unclear or nontransparent to the individual. The European Commission's enactment of the "right to be forgotten" speaks directly to this notion. While there is certainly much debate over the efficacy and soundness of this particular approach, the Platform Marketer is aware that the EU stepped into a gap (perceived or real) and created a support for consumers.

The CPO resource is well positioned to provide recommendations on how to bridge the gap between consumer expectation and experience, hopefully before additional legislative or regulatory action takes shape.

PRIVACY POLICY

Almost from the beginning, the posted privacy policy was heralded as a boon for consumer privacy, in that it allowed the consumer to know what was happening when interacting with the website in question. At the same time, the posted privacy policy was criticized as being too technical, complicated, and difficult to access and/or understand by the average consumer. Research showed that when data collection, use, and sharing of information were clearly presented, consumers preferred retailers that better protect their privacy.[8] However, another 2007 study at University of California, Berkeley, found that "75 percent of consumers think as long as a site has a privacy policy it means it won't share data with third parties." So, it's clear that confusion reigns and consumer interaction with the posted privacy policy has decreased. One might assume that no one other than regulators and plaintiffs' attorneys read them anymore.[9]

If that's true, it presents another opportunity. The Platform Marketer knows and understands that the consumer is looking for information upon which to base decisions. Right now that information may be incomplete or based on short-term benefits (e.g., access to the site or download of the app), under the assumption that the experience benefits outweigh potential risk in the misuse of their data. That may be true, but the Platform Marketer recognizes that communicating into the customer relationship is what helps

---

[8] Alessandro Acquisti and Janice Tsai, Serge Egelman, and Lorrie Cranor, "The Effect of Online Privacy Information on Purchasing Behavior: An Experimental Study" (Carnegie Mellon University, 2007).
[9] Robert Gorell, "Do Consumers Care about Online Privacy?" (October 2007). Grokdotcom.com citing to a study by Chris Hoofnagle, UC-Berkeley's Bolt School of Law, Samuelson Law, Technology & Public Policy Clinic, Berkeley.edu.

to drive value versus silence and hoping for desired outcomes. To be clear, the privacy policy is not a marketing brochure or sales collateral. It is meant to be a clear and accurate description of those data collection, use, and sharing practices employed to deliver value and rich experiences to the consumer. If that's how we understand its role then the Platform Marketer and team are actively seeking ways to deliver that information to consumers in different ways. Perhaps they can use less text-dependent methods, such as video, and places not necessarily fixed to a single location. Maybe instead of the privacy policy link from the bottom of the home page, the messaging can be found in all the relevant places and experiences that would be meaningful to the consumer. In the past, it was thought that the less we said about privacy the better so as not to scare the consumer. What we know today is that, in the same way that consumers have access to all sorts of pricing information when shopping, they also have access to information about data breaches or privacy missteps by some of the most recognizable brands in the marketplace. They are forming their own opinions and considering where they can take action. The Platform Marketer would rather tell the brand's story directly to the consumer than have someone else do it and end up with a confused—or worse, disengaged—consumer.

"One of my concerns is that lawyers have been a little bit too involved in this space," said FTC Commissioner Julie Brill. "They don't have to be thrown out of the room, but I would really like to see the creative people play more of a role in figuring out how to communicate with consumers in a layered, just-in-time way, so consumers can learn what they need to know."[10]

While she uses slightly different language, we think that Brill is really talking about ensuring that the Platform Marketer and the team are devoting time, attention, and resources to a broader-than-typical set of stakeholders, all aligned to the mission of communicating with consumers beyond what was traditionally accepted.

ADDRESSABILITY AND THE PLATFORM MARKETER

The Platform Marketer has assembled the team, covering all the key bases from privacy, legal, and data security to a user experience special-ist, providing advice about the presentation and personalization of

---

[10] www.advertisingweek.com/replay/#video-data=147.

information in the privacy context. All of this is designed to prepare for the opportunity presented by the always-on consumer and the rise of the addressable audience platform, bringing customized audiences at scale into reach like never before.

Identity Management

Often when we talk about identity, we think of name, address, race, gender, and social linkages as those bits of information that speak to our unique nature and divide us one from the other. In the context of addressability, identity management does not mean the Platform Marketer must know the customer in that context, nor does it mean that the customer is simply the sum of basic attributes. Instead, it should mean the connection of the various states of identity (e.g. offline—physical address; online—cookie ID; demographic—homeowner; device ID—tablet) with a unifying element that allows for the management of the attributes and behaviors at the individual level. This important unique identifier allows rich, meaningful, and desired experiences to be delivered to the customer no matter the channel, the medium, or the screen.

In the context of the first-party relationship with the customer, the Platform Marketer can and should know as much as possible, with the understanding that this is a give and get relationship. Give respect and trusted experiences and get information about the customer that drives insights through analytics and is then useful in future and ongoing engagements. The Platform Marketer and team have done the work to ensure that each relevant point of data capture is appropriately "noticed" and "choiced" for the consumer and that transparency and control become and remain part of the value proposition. If certain expectations have been set for consumers that would limit the use of their data for purposes outside those expectations, the Platform Marketer must adopt a plan of action for how to respect those limitations with the least impact on the business. This means either keeping that data segregated from broader, unauthorized use, or more beneficially, looking for ways to engage those customers, gain their trust, and ultimately gain consent for the broader or repurposed use of their data. The Platform Marketer is keen to avoid the traps of "unfairness" or "misleading" when thinking about leveraging customer data for potentially broader or substantially different uses.

The Platform Marketer understands that this work is designed to enable integrated and individually personalized experiences at scale and, ultimately, when and where the customer wants them. This transition from product- or campaign-focused communications to a customer-first approach must deliver on the promises made to consumers in exchange for their data. Those promises rest on the core principles of notice and choice and security and will increasingly incorporate the concept of access (i.e. transparency) into the value equation in order to drive trust.

Email Addresses

In the past, the question "What is an address?" would be fairly simple to answer. It was very likely that this data point represented the piece of information that directed someone or something to a physical location where the consumer would reliably be found. Postal address is a great example. But what happens when that construct is expanded, and the notion of reliably finding the consumer is disconnected from a physical or fixed location? That's the question the Platform Marketer is now embracing. Traditionally, the email address is thought of as a mechanism to communicate from one to many on an individual basis into a specific and unique location: the email inbox. Today, with the rise of the addressable audience platform, the Platform Marketer knows that the email address is much more than that; it is a link between two unrelated environments that can trigger messaging and engagement in a form beyond the standard email message (e.g., display advertising or Twitter messaging).

This is a very exciting opportunity, but the Platform Marketer knows that there are a number of considerations that must be addressed. Do I have permission to use the email address (i.e., PII) in this context? Is there anything in my privacy policy or at the point of collection that would have set the expectation with the consumer that this broader use is not permitted? Considering that privacy policies were generally written well in advance of this capability and may have been written to address the concern over the perception of unfettered sharing of PII, there likely may be language similar to this: "Under no circumstances do we share your personally identifiable information with third parties." If that language is a part of the Platform Marketer's privacy policy, perhaps the conclusion can be drawn that using that information to find that customer on a social media platform is likely restricted or prohibited. But the marketer may have a solution. The process of using an email address to match a user in one environment to the same user or member in another environment can be accomplished without relying on the transfer of PII. The use of a high-quality hashing algorithm can transform the email address into a hash that can then be compared to another hash of the platform's member to determine if the hashes match. If they do, there is a high probability that the same individual is present in both environments and is then placed into a customized audience that can receive that tailored messaging from the brand.

When the Platform Marketer is extending these trusted experiences into the addressable platform space where, as we know, the customer is spending more and more of his time, it is important for the marketer to ensure that these efforts are in line with customer expectations, along with any regulatory or industry-imposed codes of conduct that may apply.

Certainly, our review of the privacyscape illustrates how complicated it can be to navigate the thicket of state, federal, and industry regulations and laws, both here in the United States and around the world. The Platform Marketer is constantly reminded that, while the online space is truly borderless and the customer can come from anywhere, the rules of the road governing data collection, use, and sharing can be conflicting, confusing, and not always obvious. It's the legal resources on the team that can be charged with helping to unwind this knot.

The Platform Marketer knows that having a close working relationship with the legal and/or compliance team is critical. They are the ones who will spot the issues, provide visibility into where the do-not-cross lines are, and help craft solutions that meet business objectives in those situations where the lines are less obvious or settled (e.g., can protected health information as defined by HIPAA ever be made anonymous?).

Overall, the key deliverables to the Platform Marketer from the team would include the development of operating procedures for online and offline data collection, use practices, outsourcing, and partnering arrangements that support the business objectives. This should be seen through several lenses:

- Advancements and innovations in technology.
- The proliferation of media platforms through which the Platform Marketer can find, communicate, and engage with customer audiences.

- Multijurisdictional requirements.
- Changes in consumer behaviors and expectations.

What is the privacy and compliance action plan for the Platform Marketer? First, assemble the team and call them to action; it's never too early to start. Engage them early and often. Set goals for continuous improvement in team intelligence on key metrics like advertising technology and consumer acquisition and retention strategies. Understand the impact of macro or external factors on the business as a whole. For example, long-term decline in foot traffic to physical store locations, coupled with increasing traffic to the e-commerce site, results in less advertising in local print publications and greater investment in display, search, and mobile advertising.

The Platform Marketer knows that the integration of consumer privacy and all of its facets into the customer acquisition and retention strategies will beneficially shape the customer journey and help deliver on that core promise of rich, tailored, and personalized experiences in multiple media and channels across devices.

Chapter 7 Media Optimization

Special Contributor: Megan Pagliuca

As advertising technology has evolved over the years, the methods by which we buy and sell media have changed drastically. Technology enables the use of data and analytics within media, giving rise to the world of platform marketing. Competitive advantage is now created by a marketer's ability to leverage first-party data in media to personalize content for customers and prospects. Technology enables marketers and agencies to connect with publishers easily, and at unprecedented scale, to target the right individual with the right message in the right context. This method of media buying is defined as "programmatic."

This chapter focuses on media optimization, which is the continuous iteration of improving media performance in market. More specifically, it covers the base knowledge required and best practices for buying and optimizing digital media campaigns, with a focus on how programmatic can be used throughout the process.

First, we review the evolution of advertising technologies, followed by their impact on each of the market constituents: marketers, agencies, intermediaries, and publishers. We then review the foundational knowledge and best practices for optimizing media today, including the methods by which media is bought, the tactics used to buy it, the ad decisioning process, inventory quality, and pricing models. Finally, we highlight the market challenges we see in adoption of programmatic media.

The media planning process, which can be greatly improved by leveraging insights from first-party data and programmatic media, is out of the scope of this chapter. Search optimization is also beyond its scope.

EVOLUTION OF ADVERTISING TECHNOLOGIES

It's important to understand how advertising technology has evolved in recent years. During the early stages of display media, marketers worked directly with publishers to buy ad placements on their websites. An agency rep would pick up the phone and call Yahoo!, agree on a price, and fax an insertion order (IO). Any optimization that happened was controlled by the publisher and was primarily based on clicks. The challenge was that an agency could only manage a limited number of publisher conversations, negotiations, and IOs. The Internet was less fragmented than it is today. There were fewer websites on which consumers could spend their time; today, there are more than 1 billion websites. But it was still a challenge to get broad reach and spend large budgets. It was very difficult for mid-tier publishers to monetize their inventory, because they weren't large enough to warrant the time and operational burden of being added to the marketer's media plan. It was ideal for the large portals like AOL and Yahoo!, as they, along with other top portals, received the majority share of the online ad spend. For marketers to access greater reach and for mid-tier publishers to monetize their inventory, ad networks were created to offer a solution. Ad networks would go to the mid-tier publishers, aggregate inventory, and often build niche inventory bundles to resell. The ad network also offered optimization services, but with the goal of maximizing its own margins, rather than the advertiser's ROI. They differentiated their offerings on industry or market niche, service quality, and technology. Differentiation based on data and insights didn't come into play until much later.

As dollars started to flow more quickly into the space, inefficiencies surfaced, and ad networks resold inventory through each other, with each network taking a markup, a concept known as "daisy chaining." A marketer would place a buy with a network and that network would resell the impression to another ad network, which would resell to another ad network, and so on. With a markup at each of these steps, a marketer could be paying a $10 cost-per-thousand (CPM) and less than a dollar would go to the publisher. In 2006, the typical daisy chain went through as many as 20 different intermediaries. Inefficiency and fraud were rampant.

The inefficiency in the market exposed an untapped opportunity to create a better model. In response to this, in 2006, Right Media launched the concept of the ad exchange, which led to the broader industry adoption of programmatic media, defined as buying media through automation enabled by technology. The vision was to simplify and automate the process, so that marketers and agencies could directly link with publishers to buy an ad impression, in real time, with impression-level bidding. The Right Media technology platform allowed buyers to control which impressions were purchased at what price. The creation of a self-serve tool for an advertiser and a self-serve tool for a publisher enabled advertisers to create direct connections through "linking." A simple analogy: On LinkedIn, you create connections with business contacts; likewise, marketers and agencies can create connections with publishers for media buying relationships. The advertiser tool and the publisher tool were connected to enable automation of the IO process and the ability to decide which impression to buy at what price based on an algorithm, which we will cover in the media optimization section.

The next evolution of technology continued on this path, with a self-serve tool for publishers to monetize their inventory, known as a supply-side platform (SSP), and a self-serve tool for advertisers to buy the right impressions at the right price, known as a demand-side platform (DSP). These were separate technologies connected by a new industry protocol known as real-time bidding (RTB). Similar to linking, the ability to create direct connections was enabled between marketers and publishers, leading to what is known as private marketplaces. A private marketplace is simply a connection between a marketer or agency with a publisher that enables ongoing media transactions, similar to a connection on LinkedIn. Today, DSPs enable marketers and agencies to own ad decisioning and control over which impressions are purchased through business rules and algorithms. The DSP is a technology partner for marketers and agencies, with business terms that enable transparency into the cost of the media.

The need has also arisen for channel-specific DSPs that specialize in mobile and video.

In parallel with the evolution of technology, agencies were evolving their model, with each agency holding company launching its own trading desk. Prior to 2008, most agencies didn't have the platform marketing skill sets necessary to optimize media. They also were being squeezed on revenue by the marketers' procurement departments and saw an opportunity to take some of that margin back for themselves. They began by creating a specialized center of excellence—the trading desk—that operated much like an ad network. Trading desks are separate companies, with distinct P&L responsibility, which provide media services to sister agencies within the agency holding company family.

The top publishers struggled with the advent of RTB, as it allowed budget to be allocated easily across millions of mid-tier publishers, and the auction model, in some cases, resulted in lower prices than their historical rate cards. Top publishers were losing audience because of inventory fragmentation (more sites means more places to go). The smart publishers adopted programmatic technology and built proprietary data sets, with an understanding that their own first-party data is the new differentiator in media.

In 2012 and 2013, Facebook and Twitter doubled down and focused on their advertising offerings. This radically changed the landscape of the display market overall, and particularly the mobile media market. While they both provide RTB-based advertising offerings that can be bought through DSPs, marketers must go through an application program interface (API) developer in order to access their own first-party data bundled with their inventory. Facebook and Twitter operate in an environment that requires logged-in identity, so the accuracy and richness of their data is vastly better than in the exchange media environments. The logged-in identity spans devices, enabling them to provide tracking and measurement against mobile media spend, where the rest of the industry has a major gap. Facebook and Twitter have also led the market by revolutionizing the ad formats in mobile and tablet. Facebook in particular is redefining mobile advertising in terms of ad formats, creating targeted, rich offerings at scale. The rest of the publishers in the market are following Facebook's lead. This is the next step of the evolution in the advertising technology market.

The transactional environment for media has improved drastically for two reasons. The first is that marketers can easily reach audiences at scale across all publishers from the top tier, mid tier, and long tail. Now, any mom and pop site with great content can monetize inventory easily by plugging into an exchange environment. The second is that with the new model, transparency has been brought to the ecosystem. The days of daisy chaining multiple players and having non-value-add ad network inter-mediaries are almost gone. While many black box ad network offerings still exist within both the agency trading desk and ad tech world, a better option has been created that the leading marketers are leveraging.

MARKETER IMPLICATIONS OF THE AD TECH EVOLUTION

The evolution of advertising technologies has not only improved efficiency and transparency within the transaction but fundamentally changed the way we select, target, and reach consumers.

Audience and Context

Traditionally, agencies would select the site and placement using the site context as a proxy for audience, meaning that if a marketer was looking to target men, age 35-plus with an income of $150,000, it would place an ad on a site like Forbes.com. The evolution is about technology enabling a marketer to reach the right audience—in the right context. Now we can reach that audience across any site. Context remains important, both for relevance and in building and maintaining a brand image. An example is a marketer with a home mortgage refinance campaign that would want to show an ad next to an article about declining interest rates. The site on which the ad appears also contributes to the audience's image of the ad.

An offline comparison is a luxury marketer that locates its store in a prominent area, surrounded by other high-end retailers and ideally at the corner of the street. Women don't buy $3,000 handbags because of a relevant ad but because the brand image has been built over time. The same is true online, which is why both audience and publisher context are important.

Competitive Advantage Lies in the Use of First-Party Data

Before the evolution of programmatic media, the defining component of agency differentiation was buying clout, and competitive advantage went to the largest agencies that could negotiate the lowest prices. This caused debilitating barriers of entry for smaller agencies.

Programmatic media enables the use of data and analytics throughout the buying process. The ability to target at an addressable level is also on the rise with tactics like Facebook Custom Audiences and Twitter tailored audiences, where customer lists can be matched to Facebook and Twitter identity. While addressable targeting tactics allow us to target at an individual person level based on logged-in identity, programmatic tactics still allow more granularity than in the past, assessing at an individual impression level, which is based on the cookie. Historically, when buying broad-reach media in bulk, it was all about getting a lower price. Now, even for upper-funnel, broad-reach buys, it's about being able to use data to reach the individuals who have the right profile for your product, and to do so at the right price point. This is most valuable for marketers that already have knowledge of who their prospects should be. Take a cable television provider as an example. The marketer knows which individuals use its service, but it also knows the prospects that could potentially switch to its cable service. For that cable television provider's branding campaigns, it would want to target only those individuals. A very different industry example would be an insurance provider. For some providers, only certain individuals drive profitable policies, such as those with credit scores of 750 or more. It's critical to the marketer's business strategy that the company continues to advertise to those people with the highest potential for lucrative results.

Take the example of a large agency holding company that negotiates a block of inventory, or a first look at inventory, for the lowest price. Another agency, with the ability to use data in the process, would bid higher for an audience because of its knowledge of that audience, and could win that impression away from the larger agency. The publishers' business rules and technology should allow the highest bidder to cherry pick individual impressions based on the cookie. Competitive advantage in media buying is now about the ability to use data more effectively, and negotiation plays a lesser role.

FUNDAMENTAL KNOWLEDGE AND BEST PRACTICES

It's important to understand how to leverage programmatic technology in order to get the best results. From media buying methods to inventory quality, from analytic insights to various pricing models; due to the complexities involved, many agencies and marketers are misusing programmatic technology. The following sections review the fundamental knowledge required, as well as the best practices necessary to maximize results.

The "Plumbing" Behind Media Buying

Sophistication and complexity of buying methods have increased. While it's useful to understand at a high level, the focus should remain on the audience and the publisher and not get confused in the acronyms or the many technologies and their protocol variations. There are three primary ways of buying media, with variations within these three categories.

1. *RTB buying.* Real-time bidding is a method of programmatic buying that allows the buyers to assess what impression to purchase at what price in real time. This is ideal for the marketer because the ad decisioning is on the buy side, specifically within the DSP or channel-specific DSP platform. The challenge is that not all inventory, ad formats, and publisher data can be accessed via RTB. Through RTB, inventory can be bought directly from publishers, also known as private marketplaces, or more broadly across the open web. When buying on the open web, one can typically report on the publishers through which ads are displayed, but some sites may be masked or blocked.

2. *Programmatic guaranteed or API-driven buying.* This is a method of programmatic buying where there is workflow automation and, in some but not all cases, the use of an algorithm for decisioning. The agency will manage this through either a DSP or an API developer for Facebook and Twitter, but the ad decisioning happens on the publisher side with this type of buying. Examples include buying Yahoo! guaranteed inventory through a DSP or buying Facebook inventory through an API developer.

3. *Guaranteed media buying.* Publishers monetize their inventory directly with advertisers, without workflow automation or the use of algorithms. Publishers' custom sponsorships, content integrations, and custom ad units are mostly sold this way. Some publishers still sell standard banners this way with their high-quality inventory (quality will be defined in the next section). This is the traditional way media was bought before the advent of the programmatic method.

We can access most publishers' inventory through all three buying methods—directly, through APIs, or using RTB. Social publishers, like Facebook and Twitter, sell inventory all three ways, but inventory is primarily sold through buying platforms that access Facebook and Twitter through their APIs. This enables the platforms to keep their first-party data, and the ad decisioning can remain within their system or walled garden. We anticipate Pinterest, Instagram, and others will follow this same path. The Facebook Exchange (FBX) offering enables the purchase of inventory through RTB but without access to the actual Facebook user data. Facebook's clear priority is monetization through its API developer partner platforms, not FBX.

These are the three ways to buy inventory; they represent the different ways the plumbing actually works. The art of putting together the right media plan—and optimizing it—requires not only an understanding of the different ways to buy but also knowledge of which publishers and audiences the marketer would like to reach.

Media Buying Tactics: Remarketing and Prospecting

Remarketing is a tactic that, in some industries such as retail, is siphoned off on its own and transacted separately. Companies like TellApart and Criteo specialize in remarketing. Remarketing, or retargeting (terms that are mostly used interchangeably), refers to the practice of showing someone an ad after he or she has taken an action, like visiting a site, opening an email, clicking on a keyword, or downloading a mobile app. First-party data is leveraged in all of these examples. Remarketing can be to a current customer or a prospect, but it always involves targeting someone who has demonstrated interest in some way. Data onboarding, direct match, and custom audiences are all terms that refer to taking an offline list and matching those individuals online, then showing them an ad. These are technically forms of remarketing when first-party data is being leveraged. They represent remarketing against offline activities, such as the prior purchase of a product.

In contrast, the capability to onboard prospect lists would be a prospecting tactic. Prospecting tactics may start with first-party data but require the use of second- or third-party data for expansion. First-, second-, and third-party data are defined by relation. First-party data is data that is proprietary and gathered in one's own systems from one's own customers and prospects. Second-party data is someone else's first-party data. Buying Facebook data would be second-party data to a marketer but first-party data to Facebook. Third-party data is data that is sold by an intermediary. An example would be an online data reseller like Exelate, which might work with a travel booking website and resell "travel intenders," which would be categorized as third-party data. Another example, from offline data, would be with a data reseller like Datalogix, which could resell data from grocer loyalty programs.

For marketers, the greatest value is driven by leveraging first-party knowledge, whether it's from offline or online activity. Layering in second- and third-party data can be useful for look-alike modeling for prospecting. Third-party data can be effective to create look-alikes or refine targeting data, but there are challenges with accuracy and cost. For example, the data reseller may not be 100 percent transparent about the makeup of the data. A travel intender segment for someone who shopped for a flight to Florida in the last hour is going to be more useful than someone who shopped a month ago. Lastly, third-party data comes at a cost, which can be higher than its value. Strict ROI analysis should be used to determine the incremental lift from the data source.

An addressable tactic like Facebook Custom Audiences, where offline first-party customer lists are onboarded online, is particularly effective because Facebook operates off of a first-party cookie and leverages Facebook identity, which is based on logins. Addressable tactics can be effective in a DSP environment, but the issue is that there is a reliance on a third-party cookie, rather than logged-in identity. There are issues with third-party cookies, as they are specific to a browser, not an individual; they are sometimes deleted and reset by users and blocked by some browsers; and they are not effective in a mobile environment. In an environment like Facebook, third-party data is verified against the Facebook identity, so the example with Datalogix grocer data would likely be more accurate than buying Datalogix grocer data in a DSP environment.

In general, one should always break out remarketing and prospecting separately for reporting and measurement purposes, as the audiences are in different stages of the marketing funnel. Remarketing will always have a lower cost per acquisition (CPA), as you are converting someone who has already demonstrated interest in some way and is approaching the bottom of the funnel. Prospecting tactics are top of the funnel; you are looking to drive qualified individuals down the funnel and then convert them with remarketing. Remarketing has also become more powerful with Google AdWords' launch of remarketing lists for search ads (RLSA). Once someone visits a site, you can not only retarget them with a display ad but also customize search ad copy or change bidding strategies on keywords when that individual searches on Google. Integration between tactics is incredibly powerful. You can take an offline list of high-value prospects, onboard them online, and then drive them to the site. Once they get to the site, you can group them in a high-value segment for both search and display messaging and send custom sequenced messaging between search and display.

There are a number of tactics and data types that can be leveraged. The ability to organize business rules and algorithms to align the right content to the right audience in the right context is critical for success. Starting with the first-party data will deliver the best results.

Publisher Inventory Quality

There are multiple components that need to be considered with regard to quality: the context on the page, the responsiveness of the audience, and the viewability of the ad.

As discussed earlier, media used to be purchased using context as a proxy for the audience. With the evolution of ad technology, we can assess both the audience and the context. For context, a gasoline retailer would want to put an ad next to an article about declining oil prices. An aspiring luxury marketer would want to place ads only on high-end sites next to other high-end marketers. Then there are some types of content that most advertisers generally avoid, for example, sexually explicit content, some user-generated content, and sites that tend to create fake content just to attract advertisers. There is also a large fraud issue, where fake clicks are generated to drive growth in advertising dollars. Ad servers are, and should continue, providing tools to scrutinize content quality. But as an alternative, there are third parties that provide monitoring services that flag fraud and low-quality content after the fact and often even block it before the impression can be purchased.

The responsiveness of the audience is dependent on the relevance of the ad to the user, but in aggregate, user response rates decrease based on the depth of their session. As depicted in Figure 7.1, created by AOL, if a user

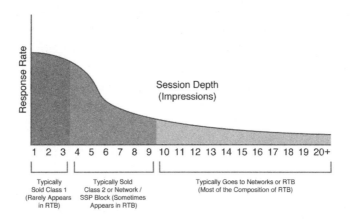

FIGURE 7.1   Session Depth in Relation to Response Rate
Source: www.slideshare.net/seattleinteractive/202-1450pm-chad-gallagher.

has just come to the site, the first ad is session depth 1, and after they have seen 20 ad impressions, they are at session depth 20. Publishers can monitor the depth of the user's session on their inventory, but do not have visibility into the length of the session beyond their site. As a rule, response rates decline as user session depth increases. The lower the frequency of depth, or the earlier the user is in his session, the higher the response rate. The low-frequency impressions can be sold for the highest CPMs, and publishers often sell directly through a guaranteed environment. The high-frequency impressions are lower in quality and are sold through exchange media environments. The high-frequency and lower-quality inventory can be referred to as "remnant."

It is true that lower-quality inventory, in terms of session depth, is typically what is sold through exchange media environments. With the evolution of programmatic guaranteed and further growth of programmatic media, we anticipate more high-quality inventory will become available to be purchased programmatically.

The viewability of an ad is also a critical component of inventory quality. We used to look at this in terms of whether the ad was "above the fold" or "below the fold" (a concept that originated with the fold of a newspaper). Buying above the fold inventory was a proxy for buying viewable impressions, and publishers would classify their inventory accordingly. In 2014, the Interactive Advertising Bureau (IAB) launched a standard for viewability, which is that 50 percent of pixels must be in view for a minimum of one second. Viewability is measured by third parties, but ultimately is a metric that should be integrated within the ad server or measurement platform. It is easiest to act upon the viewability metric in programmatic buying, because a campaign manager can optimize away from and exclude audiences and sites with low viewability. Many digital agencies and viewability leaders, like Moat and the IAB, are trying to move the industry to a standard where direct publisher buys can include a viewability guarantee.

Ad Decisioning

A marketer or agency leverages a DSP to access inventory through either type of programmatic buying, programmatic guaranteed, or RTB. Within the RTB method, the DSP has the ability to enable auto-optimization, which leverages an algorithm for the ad decisioning. The algorithm predicts in real time the value of an individual impression, based on the marketer's defined goal and the knowledge of that individual to date. The algorithm is powerful because it's acting on real-time online responses such as site visits, leads, or online conversions. For comparison, direct mail modeling may only be updated quarterly based on user response versus real-time model updates for online ads.

The algorithm is typically used in prospecting campaigns, but not in remarketing campaigns. In remarketing campaigns, the logic is just rules based. So, for example, a user comes to the site, and you want to show him an ad later in the day, so that is simply a rule. There is no need for an algorithm to decide whether to show the individual an ad or not, as we know we want to show ads to any individual who visited the site.

The dependent variable in the algorithm is the campaign goal, which is a predefined conversion metric, usually an online site visit, lead, or conversion sale. In some cases, you can also pass the offline conversions back into the algorithm. However, the algorithm performs better with more data, so it's often better to pick a more shallow conversion, like a lead, to optimize to and monitor online and offline conversions. Within the decisioning process, the algorithm checks the predicted value generated by the algorithm and determines if that is higher than the cost of the impression. If the value is higher than the maximum allowable CPM, it bids. The bid is then entered into an auction, and the marketer with the highest bid serves an ad against that impression. The algorithm is working based on the knowledge it has to date; in other words, it is determining the profiles of the individual cookies that took the action or met the campaign goal since the campaign launched. The algorithm uses variables such as originating sites, geographies, time of day, day of week, recency of ad view, and frequency of ad view to value individual cookies. Some algorithms also incorporate first- and third-party audience data to find similar audiences. The algorithm "learns," or gets smarter, as it has more data. This means the performance at campaign launch is the worst it will ever be, because the algorithm has the least amount of data. With more successful completions of the marketer's goal, the algorithm reviews more data and the cost per goal completion decreases.

A skilled campaign manager, or as some agencies refer to the role—a trader—should also be manually optimizing every campaign. The best practice for prospecting in exchange-based media is to start the campaign broad and make refinements over time. Of course, hard targeting should be in place around geography, devices, and frequency—and unproductive sites should be blacklisted—but other than that, when launching a new campaign, broad is best. Reporting should then be broken down for goal completion by publisher, technographics, third-party data segment, day part, and contextual categories. The campaign manager should see what "pops" or indexes highly against the goal and break out another line item with that target and a higher bid. It's important to increase bids for audiences that you know you want. Since it's a second-price auction, even if you bid high, you are only going to have to pay out some difference between your bid and the second highest bidder. With the Google exchange, for example, it's a penny above the second highest bidder; but this is different depending on the supply-side platform's rules. The campaign manager should always be testing higher or lower bids as the market dynamics change frequently.

This is also an auction environment, so you may be winning inventory at a given price one day, and the next day, another agency comes in with a bid on that same audience or publisher. Your performance could decline, as you no longer have access to that inventory. In the fourth quarter of the year, due to increased retailer budgets brought about by the holiday season, CPMs increase across the board. A marketer is unable to buy the inventory at the same price as the rest of the year, so campaign managers need to continuously adjust. Some demand-side platforms, like Google's DoubleClick Bid Manager and AOL's AdLearn Open Platform, are creating views that enable the campaign manager to see win rates, which would guide the campaign manager when bids must increase.

A publisher may also be selling inventory through more than one supply-side platform, or it may pull inventory out of the programmatic environment to sell directly. This is why we caution against using a supply-side platform or exchange as an optimization variable, as the inventory within the platform is not a constant.

While purchasing ads on Facebook and Twitter is similar in that media is also bought programmatically, the primary way inventory is currently bought is through platforms that access the Facebook and Twitter algorithms leveraging their APIs. The ad decisioning, or control over which user sees which ad, lies within Facebook and Twitter's algorithms, rather than within the marketer-controlled buying platform, like in exchange media buying. Facebook winners incur a displacement cost due to competition while Twitter has a second-price auction, paying just enough more to win. Both platforms factor in engagement plus user quality when bidding—a big difference from exchange media buying.

While the technology evolution, and specifically the algorithms that auto-optimize media campaigns, has enabled significant improvement in performance, the truth is an expert in optimization who understands the marketer's business could beat out even the best algorithm. An expert on the marketer's business and the platform can identify trends, learning new audiences and sites with a business context that the algorithm misses. The best results occur when we are using both the algorithm and an expert to optimize the campaign. The manual optimization, or the expert, is particularly critical with Facebook and Twitter, as there is less maturity in the decisioning algorithms. We have seen the difference between having an expert versus someone new to the platform can mean spending 10x the media budget toward the same campaign goal.

Pricing Models

For the RTB method of buying, the pricing model is a dynamic CPM (dCPM), which allows bids at variable CPM levels. Bids are predetermined by the campaign manager and dependent on the target action, such as a site visit, lead, conversion, or sale. As mentioned previously, the algorithm predicts the value of that impression against the goal. If the predicted value is higher than the maximum bid, it is entered in the auction. Because it's an auction-based environment, bids always need to be translated to a common currency, so that bids can be compared against each other and the winner can be chosen. This common currency is often known as the effective cost per thousand (eCPM). Facebook has a similar pricing model, but it's known as an optimized CPM.

It's important to note that, no matter the pricing relationship you have with any RTB vendor, whether it be a DSP or ad network, the auction works based on a dynamic CPM. The core differences between ad networks and DSPs are their different business models. An ad network will take a risk and sell on a CPA or cost-per-click (CPC) basis, while DSPs price on a percentage-of-media or revenue-share model, where the agency or marketer has transparency into the cost of the media. API providers that are leveraged for Facebook and Twitter operate with the same business model as the DSP, with a transparent percentage of media. This is a requirement mandated by Facebook for the purchase of its inventory, designed to prevent the arbitrage that ad networks commit with other publishers. Arbitrage, which was introduced in Chapter 2, is defined as the purchase and sale of the inventory at a markup. Arbitrage is not a good thing for publishers, because vendors can sell their inventory at higher prices than the publishers themselves can, effectively taking revenue from the publisher. It also has a negative impact on marketers as a large portion of their media spend is going to the ad network, which reduces the dollars they could have spent on media. In some cases, ad networks can do this because they take on the risk and sell on a cost-per-action basis. Other times they do just sell on a flat CPM. A handful of ad networks have gone public and their publicly available margins are around 40 percent, in comparison to a DSP which is 10 to 15 percent for the use of the technology platform. Note that ad networks provide "managed services," or account management and optimization services, on their platforms. DSPs and API providers offer the option of using the tech platform directly or using the managed services team for an additional percentage of media. The percentage of media for DSP managed services is usually around 10 percent.

Following is a list of the types of pricing models that vendors will offer, even though with RTB, all pricing is based on a dCPM model, and through the guaranteed method, pricing is typically on a CPM directly with the publisher.

- **Cost per lead or acquisition (CPL or CPA).** Ad network margins thrive when marketers purchase on a cost-per basis. It's important to note that publishers don't typically accept this pricing model, so if you are buying on a CPL or CPA basis, it's because an ad network is taking on the risk, but then marking up the buy. It is marking up the inventory significantly above the purchase price.
- **Cost per click (CPC).** Since search is the giant, and it evolved earlier than display, this metric, which was well understood by marketers, was translated to display. However, clicks in display do not translate into conversion metrics, so it is not a good pricing model for sales. As with CPL or CPA, ad networks take a significant markup on this model.
- **Cost per thousand (CPM).** Publishers typically sell their inventory on a guaranteed CPM basis but through dCPM with the RTB method. If a vendor is reselling RTB inventory on a flat CPM, then there is a lack of pricing transparency. Because the basic tenet of RTB buying is dynamic pricing in an auction, flat prices indicate that the vendor is buying at a lower CPM and then selling at a higher CPM. While buying from publishers on a CPM basis is the norm, it is not recommended to buy from vendors, such as DSPs or ad networks, in this way.
- **Revenue share or percentage of media.** This is the primary model for DSPs and API providers. For DSPs, the percentage of media ranges between 10 and 25 percent. In mobile, these prices tend to be on the higher side, since budgets are smaller. API providers range between 3 and 10 percent.

To get the best results, it is necessary to ensure that you have transparency on the cost throughout the process.

PROGRAMMATIC MARKET CHALLENGES

The rise in programmatic has dramatically changed the knowledge and skill sets required for digital media. The major shifts or marketer implications are that, first, we are no longer using the publisher context as a proxy for audience, but we are buying audience and publisher context. Second is that competitive advantage is now created through the ability to leverage first-party data within the process. There are challenges with the current agency model and challenges within marketer organizations that prevent adoption.

AGENCY HOLDING COMPANY CHALLENGES

The agency holding companies have attempted to take advantage of the ad technology evolution by compartmentalizing the skill sets needed to leverage programmatic into siloed organizations, known as trading desks. There are a number of problems with the trading desk model. The first is transparency around cost. Agency trading desk double dipping is well documented and is increasingly known and understood. For example, we recently consulted a large financial services marketer that was paying a percentage of media to an agency (around 8 percent) and to the trading desk (around 30 percent), and then the trading desk was leveraging the DSP managed services (10 percent). The marketer was paying almost 50 percent of media spend in service fees.

The second problem is the lack of knowledge, skill sets, and competency to leverage programmatic within the agency, since it is siloed within the trading desk. The point of programmatic is to enable an easier and more scalable connection from marketers to publishers and audiences. Yet, as an example, media plans consistently include big-name DSPs listed like any other publisher. The media plan should still be about publishers and audiences. It doesn't make sense to put an ad server on a media plan as a publisher. But a demand-side platform, which is simply a technology to connect to publishers, is often included in agency media plans.

A third challenge that is particularly problematic is that the agencies and agency trading desks lack the capability to utilize marketer-provided first-party personally identifiable information.

SUMMARY

In this chapter, we have walked through the evolution of digital media buying, from a traditional buying model that mirrored offline media buying to the current model that is real time and data driven. The market has gone from publishers being a proxy for audience to offering a real-time understanding of both person and context to drive real-time bidding. We've looked at the value that first-party data brings to the table and how starting with first-party data yields the greatest results, especially when a skilled campaign manager is in the driver's seat. We've looked at the plumbing behind ad buying and why it's important, but only because it allows us to better connect to publishers and audiences. We must not get too caught up in the technology itself. We've looked at the different media buying tactics, inventory quality, and ad decisioning techniques and pricing models. The key thing to remember across all of these components is that we are trying to bring the right message to the right person in the right place at the right time. But just as important is at the right price—this should drive optimization so that efficiency goals are met. All of the technologies that are cropping up are bringing new and innovative ways to do this. We must learn how to tease out the truth across platforms, so that we can clearly see the consumer at the end of the day and know how to have the right conversation with him at that moment. This has been the marketing dream for years, and we are coming to a point where that dream is manifesting in reality.

With $4.6 billion in 2014 spending, programmatic currently represents about 22 percent of the display market. The expectation is that it will almost double to $9.03 billion by 2017.[1]

---

[1] www.emarketer.com/Article/Advertisers-Continue-Rapid-Adoption-of-Programmatic-Buying/1010414.

Chapter 8   Channel Optimization

Special Contributor: Zimm Zimmermann

DEFINITION

What Is "Channel"?

Think of channel as the means by which a customer comes to you (as opposed to outbound interactions, delivered through media). Channel provides the means by which customers are able to make an active decision to visit your company, whether physically or virtually. They visit your website. They call your service center. They leverage an app. They even visit your brick-and-mortar location. Merkle views a channel as an avenue by which customers are able to actively elect, engage, and manage their visits and interactions between themselves and a company.

Channel aligns to any and all interactions that might occur while a customer is at your company (e.g., on your website). From sales to customer service, product to reviews, channels provide all of the necessary resources to complete whatever experience or interaction the consumer

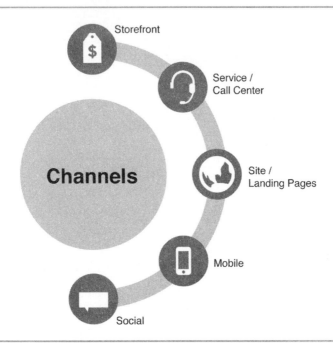

FIGURE 8.1   Channel Types

needs (see Figure 8.1). Channel optimization, therefore, is the process by which a company leverages data to manage and improve the channel to enhance customer experiences, increase interactions, and drive an increase in incremental conversions. Channel optimization focuses on incremental improvements to the consumer's experience, in order to drive high-value engagements between the brand and the consumer.

Channel optimization is not something new. Companies have been doing it since the dawn of commerce. The interior of commercial stores provide a recognizable flow and (possibly) even a branded experience. Casinos rearrange their slot machines based upon visiting guests. Service centers will route calls based upon specific customer needs. Websites are designed to simplify engagement, improve experiences, and increase conversions. Companies attempt to provide the same experience and branding regardless of channel.

But customers have moved beyond the brand and product, toward the desire for an integrated personalized experience—an experience that focuses on their specific needs. Whether on a website or at the store, customers look for personalized experiences that target their own needs and interests. They are looking for more than a product or brand; they want an experience—a conversation about the product and how that product fits their needs or how the brand is a part of their life.

Neiman Marcus has recognized the need for an integrated customer experience by enabling its iPhone app to assist in shopping for products; contacting a sales rep (via email, phone call, or FaceTime); viewing upcoming promotions and events; and more. Nordstrom has also taken the step of integrating the brick-and-mortar store with digital channels by providing such tools as a virtual dressing room, personalized homepages, and social sharing functionality. Nordstrom has provided its customers with the ability to develop, maintain, and even manage their relationship with the retailer. A relationship that will, for example, allow Nordstrom to notify them when their favorite designers' seasonal lines have arrived, which, in turn, prompts customers to stop, visit, and shop.

PERSONALIZATION

Nordstrom, like most companies today, recognizes that customers are looking for a personalized experience. Customers want companies, brands, and products to have a direct relationship with them and their needs. They are looking for a company to take advantage of the 360-degree view that the company has of them and provide a one-to-one relationship. Customers may not understand (or even know about) the buzzwords, but they are expecting a personalized relationship. In fact, the majority of customers today welcome a personalized experience.

Before we get too far along, let's take a moment to clarify what is meant by "personalization." Personalization can be defined as "the enablement of dynamic insertion, customization, or suggestion of content in any format that is relevant to the individual user, based on the user's implicit behavior and preferences, and explicit customer-provided information."

That's a rather broad statement.

By that definition alone, personalization could be something as simple as identifying customers by name during a service call or presenting them with the local weather on your website.

With such a loose definition, quite a number of companies are laying claim to personalization and their ability to provide personalization through simple rules or complex decision or recommendation engines. A small sampling of business-to-consumer and business-to-business providers

FIGURE 8.2   A Sampling of Personalization Service Providers

is listed in Figure 8.2. Some of these providers deliver personalization based on customer attributes and behavior, others based on product associations or on hybrid approaches.

On the other hand, such a broad definition offers companies the ability to expand upon personalized customer experiences. Personalization can exist within any offer, copy, creative, or call-to-action. Personalization can occur via any channel or media—a website, landing page, service center, kiosks, and so on. Personalization leverages all points of data: interaction, behavioral, attitudinal, and descriptive. It can be both obvious and obscure in its delivery. Finally, personalization can be derived by company data (implicitly) or provided by the customer (explicitly).

Personalization, in this context, enables channel optimization with the ability to develop an ongoing dialogue with the customer—a conversation. Effective conversations leverage relevant data, focused customer experiences (i.e., journeys), defined metrics for continuing the conversation, and a clear means for calculating business value.

Therefore, channel optimization moves beyond a simple performance metric for improving a desired interaction (or conversion), and becomes a comprehensive strategy focused on maintaining an ongoing relationship with each customer that visits one or multiple channels.

Channel optimization, in essence, develops a conversation between the customer and the company—a conversation that enables the company to better understand the needs, products, and services provided by the company.

CONVERSATION

In our context, a conversation is the means by which a company maintains two-way dialogue between itself and a customer, with the sole objective of helping the customer complete a desired interaction, transaction, and/or conversion. The customer defines the topic of the conversation, which can include topics such as product, services, retention, loyalty, cross-sell, up-sell, or general questions.

To simplify, personalization leverages data to manage the conversation and experience with optimized content that creates a relevant customer journey.

A conversation with each and every customer sounds like a daunting task. Yet today, companies are doing just that. In the simplest of examples, companies are optimizing their websites to personalize experiences, drive relevant offers, and increase customer satisfaction. Brands are realizing that moving beyond optimizing the average experience for all customers, via controlled testing, to optimizing the individual experience, through personalization, is driving a higher incremental performance. Personalization has moved beyond a novelty to an imperative.

MULTIVARIATE TESTING

Multivariate testing, in its simplest form, is the evaluation of one variable (offer A) versus another variable (offer B) to decide which variable has a higher level of defined interactions with the customer (see Figure 8.3). Interactions can be as simple as a click-through, opened email, or even a purchase.

Multivariate testing finds the champion between two competing variables. Once identified, the champion is leveraged for all future interactions—until such time as another challenger is introduced, at which time you start the entire process over. Some have a tendency to refer to the process as "champion/challenger" for this reason.

Multivariate testing has become a standardized business practice within all aspects of channel optimization. It has led to incremental lifts in desired business interactions as high as 30 to 40 percent. An excellent example can be found in Chapter 9, Experience Design and Creation.

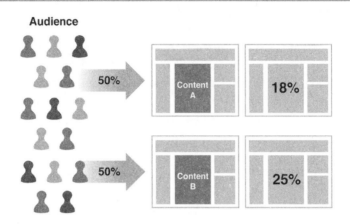

FIGURE 8.3   Multivariate Testing Scenario

SITE OPTIMIZATION

Within channel optimization, websites offer companies a bit more flexibility in the means and methodologies that can be leveraged in offering a personalized experience. Website optimization can leverage multiple offers, integrate personalization, differentiate copy and creative, segment on anonymous and known customers, and adapt the experience as the customer moves from one page to the next. We refer to this as site optimization—the practice of improving customer interactions and desired conversions within websites, landing pages, or microsites. Some types of site optimization, such as multivariate testing and usability testing (e.g., eye- and click-tracking studies), focus on optimizing the efficiency of the experience for all users as a single group. Site personalization builds on this to further optimize content in terms of messaging and delivery to the individual site visitor.

To understand the difference between optimization in a store environment versus a website, let's examine a very rudimentary example. Within the brick and mortar location, we have two different standees featuring the same product and same offer. We place them in different parts of the store. While we show an incremental lift in the sales, we are uncertain if the sales were due to the standees, and if so, which location drove the most results.

With online site optimization, our options for testing, analyzing, and adjusting increase exponentially. We have insight into the driving factors around any testing. We even have the ability to baseline the test so that each offer or message is presented on equal footing. We know:

- Who (within the addressability spectrum) is interacting with the offers.
- What offers (copy and creative) are driving customers to interact.
- Why they are interacting (e.g., because of the offer, another point within a customer's experience, or both).
- When the customers are interacting (from a time/date stamp at a point within a customer journey).
- Where the customers are interacting.
- How they are interacting (e.g., a simple conversion to a complex relationship).

Site optimization leverages the learnings of multivariate testing and the data about the customer to generate a more personalized experience.

AUTOMATING OPTIMIZATION (THE DECISION ENGINE)

Consider the number of possible touchpoints across online and offline channels and media. There are simply too many options to manually optimize the interactions one by one. The only way to do it at scale, and achieve the true potential of optimization, is with significant automation, using the right model and the right data. When automating an optimization program, we break the process down into five key phases (see Figure 8.4).

FIGURE 8.4   The Decision Engine

1. **Collect data.** The volume, variation, and velocity of data determines the richness potential of personalized experiences.
2. **Analyze the data.** Leveraging individual and group attributes, models are built to map personalized content delivery to individuals.
3. **Decide what to present.** Platforms execute the models, business rules, and machine learnings that power personalized experiences.
4. **Present.** The personalized content (copy/creative) is delivered in branded and compelling experiences.
5. **Optimize.** Models are optimized over time based upon interactions, predictive engines, attributes, and other relevant data so as to increase the desired performance or conversions.

Within the Merkle technology stack, the automation sits at the center, managing data, analysis, and content as a customer interacts and engages with a company (see Figure 8.5). Leveraging the automation process just described, we can walk through a sample of how automated optimization manages a personalized experience with a customer.

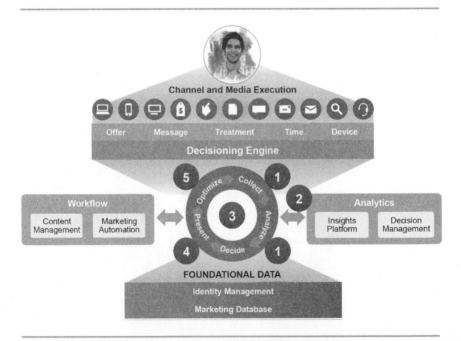

FIGURE 8.5   The Marketing Technology Stack

- As an individual visits the channel (site), data is collected to identify the individual. The data can range from the few attributes that we are able to glean from the person's IP address or browser user agent to corresponding information that we have about him within our foundational data (i.e., identity management and marketing database).
- Once we have identified who the visitor is and what we know, we leverage predefined models, rules, and analytics derived from decision management to power the automated optimization process.
- Leveraging the data, rules, and analytics, the automated optimization engine determines the most appropriate interaction for the customer. In some cases analysts may override or inform the engine recommendations based on business rules, example-specific offer suppression based on eligibility criteria, and so on.
- With the recommendation decided, content (both copy and creative) are selected from the content management solution and executed via the defined channel to deliver a personalized experience to the customer, which is targeted to her needs and interests.
- Upon delivery, the site collects additional data on the consumer's interactions, conversions, and nonresponses, so as to optimize and manage the ongoing customer conversation. Testing is also built into this process to allow the introduction of new offers, products, treatments, and messages into the personalization process.
- This is what we consider true personalization: personalization that leverages relevant data, insight/analysis, and targeted content to deliver an optimal experience, message, and interaction, thus developing and maintaining an ongoing conversation with the customer. Looser definitions of personalization (e.g., basic channel-specific product recommender engines or simple experience modification based on explicit customer-provided data) are still incorporated into developing and managing the overall customer experience.

SCALES OF TARGETING

When we look at the differences in channel optimization techniques, we can see the true impact of personalization and automation. When a company opts not to do any form of targeted marketing, the incremental lift in business value is negative, causing a detrimental impact to a company as can be seen in Figure 8.6.

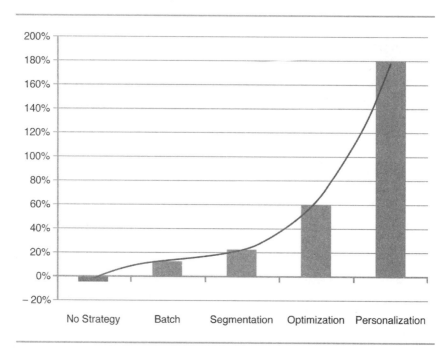

FIGURE 8.6   Conversion Ratio to Level of Targeting

Basic batch targeting and segmentation will provide a small incremental lift. With the right analytics and closed-loop marketing processes, these methodologies can be extremely beneficial in helping a company understand its target, segments, and approach to content. It is not until a company begins to employ optimization strategies that it sees a significant incremental lift in business value from combining foundational data, customer engagements, marketing analytics, and decision management. Optimization has proven time and time again to be a key component in refining channel programs. In another chapter, a clear case will be made as to why optimization is a core component of personalization.

Personalization is the most advantageous next step after optimization. While a company can continue to work and improve upon its optimization program, in general, it will only see small incremental improvements after the initial deployment of its optimization program. Personalization takes a company's channel optimization program to a new level of customer experience, content development, and incremental lift in business value.

Personalization's reliance upon decision management and workflow gives credence to the phrase "content is king," and personalization is the only means by which to manage the automation of the right message, right channel, right time, right person principle.

CONTENT CONSIDERATIONS

The reality here is that content is going to be needed, a lot of content. Content development for personalization is an extensive topic, one that could fill a whole book. For the moment, let's focus on what our automated system requires of its content in order to deliver on the needs of personalization and also inform future content development.

The content must anticipate a personalized moment. Indeed, it must anticipate *all* the possible personalized moments. This means we need a deep understanding of both the customer perspective as well as those critical touchpoints that benefit from personalization before any content development can begin. This will vary depending on the industry. In e-commerce those moments are closer to the point of purchase, but when choosing a life insurance policy, personalization can be even more effective in the consideration stage. Detailed experience maps are helpful when planning content development for personalization, as they can identify and prioritize the moments it will be most effective.

The content must be flexible and modular. Keeping message, offer, and treatment separate and interchangeable gives us the ability to stretch the variations that can be delivered. And the order that messages can be displayed gives us even more variation. Simply displaying the benefit of a product before the offer is a form of personalized variation and vice versa—what we know about a customer helps us determine which order will be most effective for conversion.

The content must to be compelling. This means it must be both high in quality and very relevant for the personalized moment. Many forms of personalization simply reflect a previously viewed product or state an obvious step in a purchase process, which can have its benefits. But extending what is possible in personalized content by supplying more contextual elements (anticipating time of day, using previous behavior to simplify an action, using customer loyalty to incentivize in real time) can be even more influential for the customer engagement.

GETTING STARTED

We see a specific set of components and means by which to move a company from a simple "batch and blast" to a fully personalized channel optimization program. Our approach: Develop a customer strategy program that can take advantage of both the customer experience design and powerful learning capabilities of automated optimization.

- Develop the right mix of copy and creative, specifically designed to create and manage ongoing one-to-one consumer interactions.
- Develop, manage, and optimize custom analytics and models that provide the support and learnings associated with an automated personalization engine.
- Know and understand the integration and management of the data flow.

Once there, we can begin with the creation of customer journeys and personalization use cases to inform the broader personalization strategy. Strategies turn into detailed strategic conversations with a defined implementation plan as shown in Figure 8.7.

Next, we look at the data integration and event stream development (Figure 8.8). We begin with the creation of event streams across anonymous and known consumers. This event stream creates engagement "memory" across touchpoints—a first step to connecting otherwise disconnected customer interactions into a conversation.

Finally, we align channel optimization (Figure 8.9). Event streams are fed into an analytic and rules engine to determine the right communication packet (treatment, offer, device, and timing) for each consumer

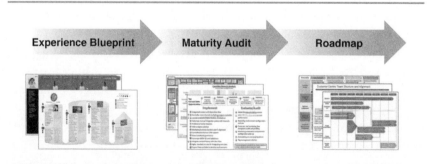

FIGURE 8.7   Sample Implementation Plan

Consumer Event Stream

User ID	Date Time	Event ID	Event Description
1234	2/1/12	DM437	DM Delivered
1234	2/2/12 3:05 PM	DI9076	Display Impression
1234	2/2/12 3:06 PM	CC068	Inbound Call Center
1234	2/2/12 5:05 PM	EM087	Sent Email
1234	2/2/12 9:30 PM	EM088	Opened Email
1234	2/2/12 9:30 PM	EM089	Clicked Email
1234	2/6/12 9:00 PM	PS674	Purchase
1234	2/6/12 9:15 PM	Q8740	App Download

Event Meta Data

Event ID	EM088
Creative	A2346 Connecting your Samsung TV and Tablet
Offer	O192365 Free Milk song download
Product	P978 Samsung PN45321

FIGURE 8.8   Data Integration and Event Stream Development

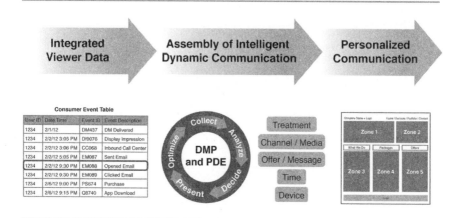

FIGURE 8.9   Channel Optimization Alignment

touch. Ongoing oversight of the optimization program ensures that personalization provides a continued, incremental lift in business value and improves messaging effectiveness.

These three steps provide the foundational aspects of a channel optimization program that focuses on the customer's journey, channel optimization, and personalized consumer conversations.

SITE OPTIMIZATION SAMPLE

In our experience, personalization is being used to manage several different pages throughout an entire website, and predefined zones within each of those pages as shown in Figure 8.10.

Each zone contains defined business rules and objectives, customer journey purpose and integration, unique content (copy/creative) associated with the zone, and optimization criteria and methodology. However, as you can see in Figure 8.11, within Zone 1, personalization is optimizing on more than one simple aspect of the zone.

Personalization optimization occurred on the (A) offer, (B) creative, and (C) call-to-action. This level of optimization requires:

- Increased collateral, which is simplified through a direct connection to the content management platform.
- The right foundational data to be used by the decisioning engine in determining the right conversations, interactions, and experience.

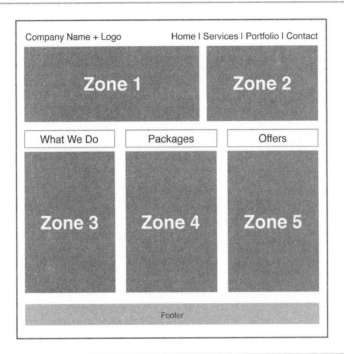

FIGURE 8.10   Personalization Zones

Personalized Content:

A Message / Offer

B Creative / Treatment

C Call-to-Action

FIGURE 8.11   Personalization within Zone 1

- A detailed customer journey with predefined conversion points that move the person through the experience while maintaining the personalized conversation.
- Ongoing analysis and optimization.

CHANNEL OPTIMIZATION HAS CHANGED

Over the past 25 years, Merkle has analyzed channel optimization. We have watched the growth of the digital realm and the impact that data is having upon all of the channels. From optimization to personalization, we realize that the level of customer engagement is growing. Consumers want companies to know who they are and what they want, and they expect targeted, personalized experiences.

Chapter 9 Experience Design and Creation

Special Contributors: Patrick Collins and Kevin Walsh

Nothing is more provocative among creative professionals right now than the role of data and analytics in the creative process. A recent headline in *Ad Age* proclaimed that "Data-Driven Creative Equals Mediocre Creative." In our experience, nothing could be further from the truth—and now more than ever, as the concepts of customization, personalization, and addressability at scale become a reality through the proliferating digital audience platforms.

In this chapter, we will highlight the benefits of bringing together the right-brain and left-brain capabilities of experience design and show how data can be used to elevate your creative. When executed well, data and analytics will: accelerate the creative process, provide a shortcut to known truths, improve the quality of ideas, and allow for less campaign waste.

How often have you clicked the unsubscribe link on an email because the copy didn't resonate or was clearly targeted to the wrong person? It is blatantly irresponsible for creative professionals to disregard what the data exposes. Data provides visibility; visibility provides insight. With insight, we can make fewer assumptions, create more impactful campaigns, and improve business performance. Improvements can be made to your creative and experience design process by:

- **Creating with insight.** Start with a more informed creative brief.
- **Optimizing constantly.** Launch and iterate; it takes a minute to learn and appreciate it and a lifetime to master.
- **Developing unique creative for targeted audiences.** Custom creative for different customer segments will always drive better results.

Let's explore each of these concepts in more detail.

CREATING WITH INSIGHT

Most marketers are familiar with the concept of a creative brief (Figure 9.1). Many projects start off with one, but few end up with exceptional results. Why does this happen? Often briefs are too focused on the functional benefits of a product rather than on the influential aspects of the consumer. Briefs tend to generalize audience information to mere demographics and assumed attitudes. They may be factual, but they don't provide enough insight for a creative team to shine. Spelling out the components of a marketing initiative is only part of what a creative team needs to be successful.

WHAT MAKES A GREAT CREATIVE BRIEF?

Exceptional creative requires more than just a general audience landscape. To market effectively, the brief should contain clues to what will most positively influence customers to respond. Those clues come in the form of customer brand perception, buying motivations, and other decision factors that run through a customer's head when considering a product or brand.

Key Characteristics of a Worthy Creative Brief

- It's short, never more than two pages.
- It advises on what you need the consumer to think, feel, and do.

Date: 02/10/14
Job Number: 153-19457
Job Name: Card Flyer Presence

Overview:

Item	Details/Comments
Client	Waterfall Clothing
Client contact	John Smith
Deliverable(s)	Develop a cardmember exclusive (CME) and in-store (ISF) ad placement strategy for the Waterfall Financial retail flyer
Target audience	Existing and prospect cardmembers
Offer	There are multiple ad options throughout the flyer: • CME 1: % of all purchases • CME 2: Type of multiplier on selected products • ISF: No interest, no fee financing for up to 12 months on purchases greater than $200
Channel	WC Retail Flyer
Creative sent to client	03/08
Presentation date	03/10

Background:

Overview:

The WCR flyer has extremely high readership (11M weekly distribution) and therefore provides a key opportunity to communicate with existing and potential cardmembers.

• Existing cardmembers: the flyer ad serves as a compelling reminder that the Options Mastercard card (OMC) provides a substantial amount of added value when shopping at Waterfall Clothing. By not using it, cardmembers are "leaving money on the table."
• Prospect cardmembers: the flyer ad could compel them to seek out acquiring a card because they realize how much added value they are missing out on.

WC has been very successful over the last few years in integrating into the weekly flyer. Unfortunately, if you look at the current opportunities (see examples), it's quite overwhelming and confusing. There doesn't appear to be a strategy for the how, when and where the various ads are presented. This includes formats, colors, fonts, logos, etc. As a result, they are asking for our help to answer these questions and better leverage these opportunities.

Challenge:

Help WC better leverage their current flyer CME and ISF opportunities by doing the following:
• Develop a recommended ad placement strategy for CME and ISF ads going forward
• Develop an integrated creative approach for featuring CME and ISF ads

Creative Objective:
• Ensure we are maximizing response for the current flyer opportunities from both a usage and acquisition perspective

Creative Insights:
• Ad placement strategy should include:
  - Recommendation for ad type (CME or ISF) based on type of products being featured
  - Simplify the number of ads the retail group has to choose from, as the placement opportunities present themselves

FIGURE 9.1   A Typical Creative Brief, Light on Real Customer Insight

- It suggests a competitive advantage.
- It provides a customer insight or perspective.
- It advises on the best ways to motivate a customer response.

Of the five criteria listed, the first three are generally achievable by a capable marketing leader. But the last two pose a bigger challenge. They require a rigorous investigation process—plus the skills to decipher what the investigation uncovers.

Your marketing strategies require more than just demographic and purchase behavior data to build effective messaging. You also require a deep understanding of what drives a consumer decision. Within any customer decision is a core motivational element that must be identified early in the creative process (see Figure 9.2). Often the factors that motivate a customer come from specific hidden personal values. Consider your choices for customer research carefully. Do your methods include investigation into motivational factors? Your ability to discover what the targetable population requires to make a purchase decision creates a big advantage in both message and treatment of your marketing experiences.

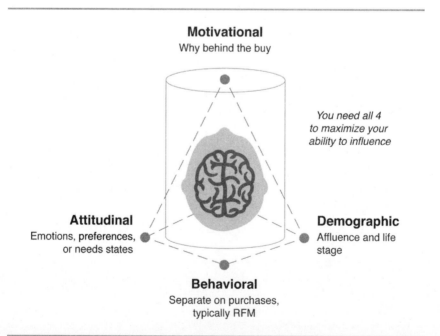

FIGURE 9.2 Four Dimensions of Audience Profiling

CONVERTING CUSTOMER INSIGHT

Uncovering the insights is only the first part of the effort. Connecting those insights to better performing marketing initiatives is the real challenge for the Platform Marketer. Besides a team that has the ability to *find* the right insights, a process is required to *translate* them into marketing strategies and tactics and to socialize them through the rest of the organization. Consider the following steps to transform customer insight into focused marketing moves:

1. Frame the problem.

    Before beginning any customer investigations, you should identify general market needs, examine competitive dynamics, determine areas of growth potential, and gain stakeholder alignment on important business needs or operational constraints.

2. Perform qualitative investigation.

    Take the framed problem and focus on the motivational aspects of customer purchase decisions. Develop a discussion guide for the interviewing process that guides the conversation toward the values that influence customer decisions.

3. Perform quantitative leveling.

    Through analytic modeling techniques, you can then determine the prevailing customer sentiment in your audience by conducting specialized surveys that are crafted from the raw material of the qualitative findings.

4. Visualize the results.

    In order to get team alignment and actually see the findings from the qualitative and quantitative exercise, you'll need to tie product features and benefits to the personal emotions and values of your customers. The best way to do that is to show the connections. Using the data from the qualitative leveling you can also emphasize what is most important to your audience. The connected decisions diagram in Figure 9.3 shows how product attributes connect to customer values during purchase decisions.

5. Translate the findings.

    Using the map, you can now discern the various groups of customer types that align to different motivational factors. You can then build customer personas and profiles to illustrate your discoveries. Figure 9.4 illustrates customer profile aspects, including motivational factors, barriers to conversion, brand alignment, and key message strategy.

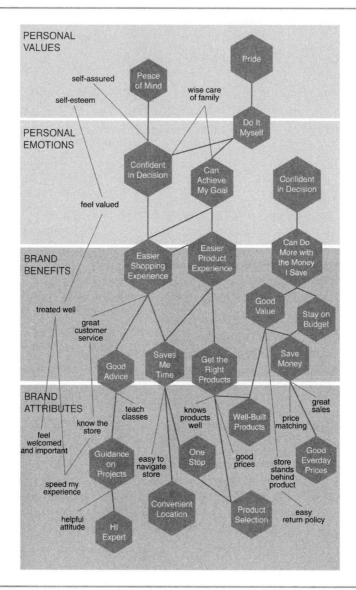

FIGURE 9.3   Connected Decision Diagram

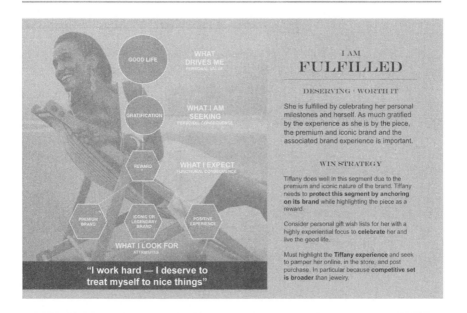

FIGURE 9.4   Customer Profile

Now you can combine demographic, attitudinal, emotional, and motivational details into the distinct customer profiles and develop marketing objectives, unique positioning strategies, and sets of penetration tactics—all based on motivational factors.

6. Feed the creative brief.

Now, the creative brief can be pumped up with clearer direction on how to best influence the customer. Instead of simply mentioning attributes of a particular audience, we can now suggest things like better language choice, words to avoid, message focus, even focused thematic elements. This will establish a better foundation for our creative ideas and marketing tactics. Figure 9.5 is an excerpt from a brief that indicates language, thematic suggestions, and other areas for creative consideration.

BEYOND THE BRIEF

As expected, these actionable insights become even more powerful after the creative phase, when it is time to get into optimization. The work that

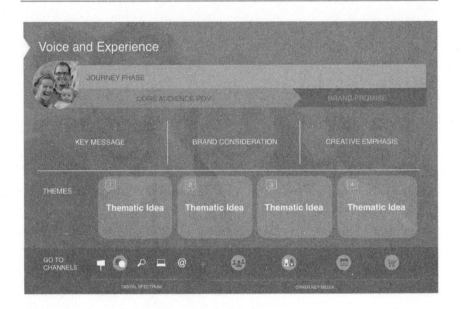

FIGURE 9.5   Areas for Creative Consideration

went into improving the brief can also set up how test plans are designed. Knowing what motivates distinct types of customers gives the perspective needed to measure performance in content choices, message variation, functional steps, and other forms of experience optimization.

OPTIMIZING CONSTANTLY

A new movement called "agile marketing" has recently emerged, which crisply captures many modern marketing best practices. Among other things, agile marketing promotes the ideas of validated learning over opinions or conventions and adaptive, iterative campaigns over big-bang campaigns.

In order to embrace these two ideas of validated learning and iterative campaigns, Platform Marketers must be willing to assume that their initial creative ideas—even though better informed through data-driven insights—will need to be adapted in market. While this may sound very obvious to many, the counter force is that many creative processes do not support this approach, and many creative teams are not well trained to work this way. Many creative professionals are unwilling to revisit prior decisions or indeed during the creative process, to admit that they don't know which creative will perform better.

Adopting a willingness to be constantly optimizing requires a different perspective on how to approach the creative process. It requires brands to engage their creative agencies differently as well. It means that the creative process can't be developed in a vacuum but, instead, must be an integral part of the ongoing marketing operations.

In nearly all businesses, optimizing the customer experience is central to successful conversion. This means that, as a Platform Marketer, you require a culture that makes it a priority to uncover friction wherever it lurks and has a dedicated process for fixing it. It's important to note that this will be different across varying business models—so the steps to take may change, but the cultural values remain the same, regardless of industry. Following are steps you may want to consider.

- **Build a creative testing culture.** Optimization can only succeed in a culture that understands that this is a constant process. Friction is guaranteed to creep back into your customer experience if neglected. A good creative testing culture means no one gets disenfranchised. All experience owners must have a voice during test planning. However, the reality is that 99 percent of optimizing decisions reflect the opinions of the most senior people in the room; the HIPPO (highest paid person's opinion) rules. This usually causes an underestimation of the situation, which results in performing fewer tests, misguided testing goals, or worse, an avoidance of a known creative issue. This is damaging, because it delays real testing. And as marketers, given the pace at which we are running to keep up with friction, we can't afford to be wasteful with our time.

- **Avoid starting with a heavy redesign.** A typical HIPPO approach is to start over or be dramatic with a design. Be aware of the pitfalls of a heavy design phase. Before you go deep on a redesign, do smaller tests to assess the impact of your thinking. The result may be different than you think. And you may be able to avoid many design cycles by experimenting with what you have in its current state. Instead of a dramatic redesign, consider quick, deliberate tests. You will be surprised what you learn about your assumptions as to where the friction exists.

- **Be polarizing with your tests.** The best testing experiments succeed when there are extremes at play. Try distinct variations to draw out customer preference. For example, move your button all the way to the opposite side, or change your imagery to reflect a completely different mood. The finding may be that customer behavior may not change at all. Button placement or site imagery may not matter at all to the customer experience. The friction may lie somewhere else. A nonresult is still a result; it tells you not to spend time changing it.

- **Be brave with your testing.** Let's be honest, the majority of tests may fail. The important thing is to never stop until there is an answer. A healthy testing culture rewards the courageous people who continue to ask the right questions.

- **Be patient waiting for the results.** There is a sweet spot in testing duration. It's called statistical significance, or reliability (see Figure 9.6). Know how long you need to wait for results. Incorporating analytics into your testing plans will save not only your time but your sanity. In many circumstances analytics can help to predict the point in time when statistical significance will occur and can keep you from bailing on a test before its results are proven to be accurate.

- **Begin with the biggest impacts.** Start where friction is always the biggest and work outward. You could start with things like brand treatment,

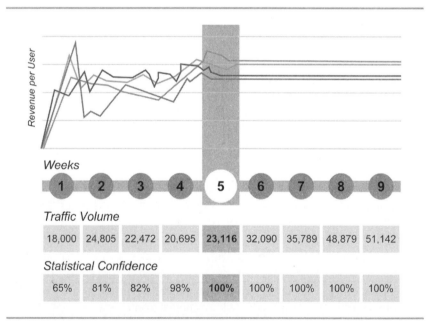

FIGURE 9.6   Statistical Significance

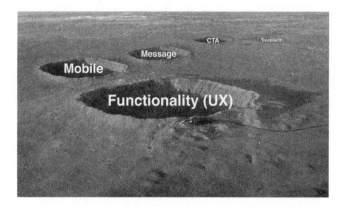

FIGURE 9.7   Consider What Makes the Biggest Impact

but it will pale in significance to mobile standards and customer interaction best practices (see Figure 9.7). So consider small, deliberate creative tests that will help inform larger friction issues.

Ultimately, this kind of testing is just one integral component of the larger optimization cycle. For instance, what can be verified in, say, a social ad test can enlighten how that creative should be represented in other places along the customer journey, like a welcome email, return site visit, or even follow-up call center scripts (see Figure 9.8). A strong testing culture will enable you to connect this kind of knowledge. And you will move faster toward reducing friction across the entire experience. All of this requires a tightly coordinated team of analytic, technology, and user experience professionals.

RAISING THE BAR

Sometimes the baseline that everyone thinks is realistic is actually the low end of what is achievable. A recent client of ours knew she needed to continue to find ways to improve the performance of a new homepage design. The challenge was that executives in the organization concluded that the performance was already great; it was achieving the results they had expected from a homepage. She was deterred from investing any more

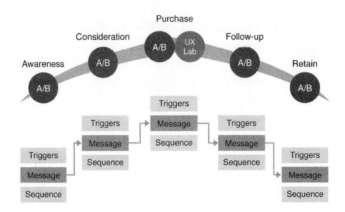

Apply learning across multiple touchpoints.

FIGURE 9.8 Connect Optimization Knowledge across the Journey

time in homepage optimization. Regardless, she was convinced she could make it much better. Bravely, she juggled some priorities around and found the resources within her existing budget to charge ahead, in spite of the naysayers, and build a new testing plan. She focused on small things like deliberate changes to form fields, adjusted imagery, and refined language. Her efforts have netted a 40 percent improvement in customer quote completion in just a few months. She has since become a hero in her office.

FINDING THE RIGHT SUCCESS

Another client tapped our agency to design a digital experience to showcase its "Family of Products"—a brand message the client hoped would result in increased sales for its lower-performing products. The new page was effective and the results were almost immediate. Each product experienced a higher conversion rate on the new landing page than it had before. Most brands would consider this creative a success and walk away. However, we were also tracking revenue effect and noticed that the net revenue impact to the business was more than a 5 percent loss! Why was this happening?

We determined this was the result of other products within the "family" not being strong enough in their messaging during the conversion cycle. As a result, they were dragging down the revenue impact of all the products represented. So, we shifted our approach to instead put optimization energy into the conversion funnel of the weaker products. The "Family" message was replaced with a new message directing customers to a landing page devoted only to the client's top product. The refocused optimization efforts have lifted the channel's sales conversion by an average of over 70 percent, resulting in a much more dramatic increase in revenue.

BREAKING DOWN SILOS

Testing and optimization means achieving the best results within the reach of your own team. Often that means optimizing within your silo, where the immediate testing culture exists, before branching out and causing unintended, far-reaching pain for the rest of your organization. But to achieve maximum advantage, this expansion should take place as quickly as possible.

We recently worked with a company whose goal was to improve the effectiveness of its media efforts by focusing on post-click–through landing pages. We redeveloped the landing pages with best practices and continued to optimize the experience to achieve higher levels of performance. Rather than isolating this performance knowledge, the client took the optimized landing page to other internal stakeholders who were relying on the same evergreen website. Everyone saw a sales improvement every time. For a brand that was already enjoying relatively high conversion rates, this was a revelation. This same team is now engaging across nearly every page of the main website to improve messaging and remove even more friction from the experience.

Many brands and agencies mistake compromise for collaboration. When we first engage with a client on an optimization project, we will always propose two drastically different ways of solving a marketing challenge. Each approach has its strengths and relies on a very likely hypothesis. The old way would be to combine the favorite aspects of each version to create a Frankenstein's monster of an experience and hope the compromises elicit the best results of both options. Instead, consider delivering both experiences, and track KPIs associated with the differences to identify the highest performing experience. Establish a better baseline this way and then incrementally add new ideas and more testing along the way.

In order to embrace creative optimization, Platform Marketers must ensure that all aspects of their operations and processes facilitate decisions based on data rather than opinion. They must be prepared to test multiple concepts concurrently. They must ensure analysts are involved early in the creative process. They must always be working on challenger creative, and most important, they must ensure that their creative teams have the time set aside to engage in post-launch optimization.

UNIQUE CREATIVE FOR TARGETED AUDIENCES

We've discussed throughout this book the benefits of personalized experiences and media targeted to individual consumers or audiences. At some point, however, the different creative advertising variations and personalized site content need to be created and trafficked, which provides unique challenges in comparison to traditional creative processes.

Targeted advertising and personalized site experiences, when done correctly, might need to target different devices, segments, or customers at different states of the purchasing life cycle. As shown in Figure 9.9, this can necessitate a massive variety of creative and content.

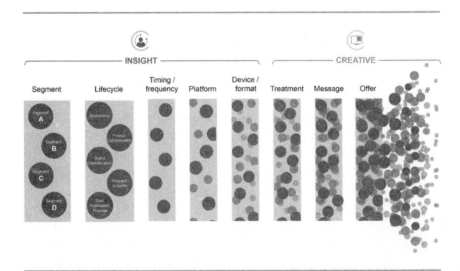

FIGURE 9.9   Targeted Media and Personalized Experiences Can Necessitate a Massive Variety of Content and Creative

The first challenge is providing a smooth enterprise workflow approval for a large number of creative variations. Often in larger enterprises, there is a sophisticated system of checks and balances on creative for regulatory or legal purposes. A large number of variations of creative can wreak havoc on approval systems. To solve this challenge, consider approving creative and copy variations in principle rather than in final form. Figure 9.10 shows a creative approval process for a single creative concept with 108 variations of creative. Using this approach to creative approval can simplify the operational challenges. This particular campaign had 5 additional creative options totaling over 600 different creative options.

A smart targeting platform like Facebook can dynamically match the right creative to the right audience. In real time, it can determine which creative is working more effectively for which audience and emphasize that creative. The Platform Marketer must encourage the creative teams to leverage the capabilities of these new targeting platforms.

In the campaign shown in Figure 9.10, the creative team was surprised by the outcome. For instance, images with solid purple-colored backgrounds performed more strongly than images with black or white backgrounds. Which direction the character faced (left or right) made a difference to the click-through rate. Even some characters performed better than others.

Creating this many variations of creative can be challenging. It's important to remember that because the environment of dynamically managed creative changes so rapidly, teams need to be amenable to *what the data tells them*. Pre-filling a number of media slots with multivariant creative is archaic. Creative teams need to understand the power of platform optimization and be willing to create individual assets that can be assembled into cohesive communications.

Imagine the cost in time and resources of attempting to create 600 or more individual creative units. Even using multiple teams to individually create these variations could be overwhelming and cost prohibitive. Conversely, a single team wouldn't have the physical capacity to create every possible variation of an ad for every single audience.

SUMMARY

The Platform Marketer can only succeed when the marketing process mandates the use of customer insights to feed creative efforts, not only at the brand level but in all engagements throughout the funnel. And

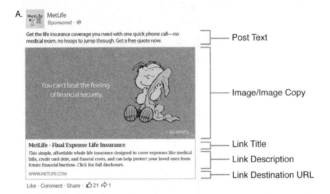

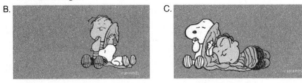

FIGURE 9.10   From Few, Many

One of six variations of creative with approximately 600 different pieces of creative.

motivational insights that examine what drives consumer purchase decisions should be included as a key component of customer strategy.

It is also critical to establish a culture where everyone strives for constant optimization. Encourage marketing teams to share testing results with each other in order to strengthen the effectiveness of the entire customer journey across the traditionally siloed marketing functions.

And finally, continue to find ways to deliver differentiated creative treatments for targeted audiences, and use platforms like Facebook to dynamically match the right creative to the right audience.

Chapter 10 Audience Platform Utilization

Special Contributor: Matthew Naeger

After assessing each of the competencies covered in the earlier portions of this book, it is time to think about how you make the most of the platform marketing stack to achieve the goals that you have set for your programs. The previous areas address key competencies that are necessary to utilize digital platforms effectively. Now we will focus on the differences between the platforms and how you can make the most of your ability to communicate in an addressable fashion with your potential, new, and existing customers.

To start, it is important to recognize that addressable platforms are changing on a daily basis. What we have today from companies like Google, Facebook, and Twitter is quickly being parroted by major publishers and merchants like Amazon, Walmart, and AOL. Additionally, each platform is racing to evolve and provide greater value to its advertisers as more money heads into the digital space. Each platform has its own set of features that helps to differentiate the value and the experience, but to this point there is

FIGURE 10.1 Audience Prioritization

not one that has become a total solution for marketers, due to the proprietary nature of the products and the audiences available to each independently. Each of the platforms is working toward the goal of one-to-one addressable audience targeting in one form or another. As that targeting continues to increase, a heightened focus is placed upon how to utilize each platform. Equally important is determining how you plan to integrate your message delivery and experiences *across* platforms when the connections between IDs and users are not synergized. In order to improve that process and unify the experience, it is necessary to start thinking about how your planning process needs to change. Figure 10.1 illustrates how to prioritize the audience in your planning process.

As you can see from the outlined process, it becomes important to be able to pull the audience experience plan into the briefing process and the media plan development for the selected platforms. With the Platform Marketer stack, you then have the ability to move audience members

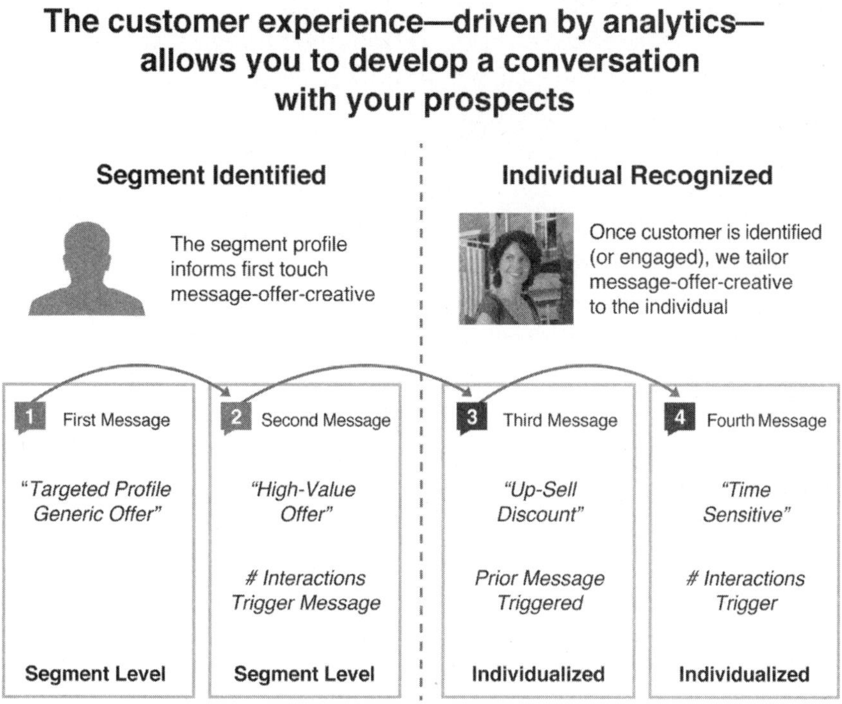

The customer experience—driven by analytics— allows you to develop a conversation with your prospects

Segment Identified		Individual Recognized	
The segment profile informs first touch message-offer-creative		Once customer is identified (or engaged), we tailor message-offer-creative to the individual	

1 First Message	**2** Second Message	**3** Third Message	**4** Fourth Message
"Targeted Profile Generic Offer"	*"High-Value Offer"*	*"Up-Sell Discount"*	*"Time Sensitive"*
	# Interactions Trigger Message	*Prior Message Triggered*	*# Interactions Trigger*
Segment Level	**Segment Level**	**Individualized**	**Individualized**

FIGURE 10.2   Message Framework Example

between messaging cycles and develop deeper experiences. Utilizing a message framework such as that shown in Figure 10.2, you can take advantage of the addressable nature of these new platforms and connect to a customer via the platforms either independently or in combination. Additionally, you can use the value segmentation of your customer data to guide the media placement process and, on a person-by-person basis, determine how much you are willing to spend on the next ad based on the expected return. Each component will hold a different value and each experience will serve a different purpose in developing your relationship with the customer.

SCALE OF ADDRESSABLE AUDIENCES

The main challenge for expanding the use of audience platforms for the past several years has been the lack of scale in the size of the audience that could be managed with multiple message scenarios. As we mentioned in Chapter 7, which looked at media optimization, media plans used to be fairly simple. First, you planned which sites you wanted to purchase. Next, you planned which networks you wanted to buy in order to expand the reach and volume of the impressions you could serve. And finally, with your remaining budget, you planned some form of a programmatic buy. Each of these tactics was typically optimized at a CPM level, and the levers that were utilized were basic reach and, possibly, engagement metrics.

As Facebook, Twitter, and Google have expanded their platform-based product offerings, they have additionally expanded the quality of the inventory and the types of ads that could be delivered. Each of these expansions has yielded better tools for understanding the audience to whom you will serve your ads and how often you can find those people. As these platforms have grown and improved, we have been given the capability to determine a number of factors prior to a buy such as:

- How many potential impressions a platform would serve to each specific audience (based on volunteered demographic data, as opposed to typical platforms, which are using third-party interpreted data).
- What types of interests those audiences have been expressing through their behavior within the platform (i.e., Google's in market targeting, Facebook's interest targeting, and Twitter's interest categories).
- How often the audiences are available.
- How much it will cost to serve ads to those audiences.

Armed with this information the media planning process can become much more outcome-based and marketers can provide ROI forecasts before media is executed.

Now that the platforms have matured, the idea of adopting an audience-first approach to media planning is pushing to the forefront of the industry. The Platform Marketer is driving this change and will continue to do so as the addressable audience platforms grow. In total scale, Facebook, Twitter, and Google have the ability to consistently reach more of the global consumer market than any other media platform. You are seeing television networks, as well as cable providers, scrambling to enable digital delivery of their programming and their advertising. Addressable video and television advertising are starting to grow to scale, and we are seeing the evolution of these same types of audience platforms enabled by digital and offline data at the individual level. As addressable television advertising and video platforms evolve, they will lead to the same type of targeting and measurement that we have on the digital platforms today. There are going to be new networks rising and new platforms fighting to win the battle of who can build and integrate the fastest. And just as you saw Google make its name in search, Facebook build its platform in social data sharing, and Twitter build its platform on the immediacy of interest-based data, you will also see a new major player emerge in this space over the next two years.

AN OVERVIEW OF THE PLATFORMS

Facebook

Anyone who uses Facebook on at least a semi-regular basis will tell you that the social network has both positive and negative features for its users. However, more than a billion people rely on it consistently to help keep in touch with their friends, find out new information, and as a source of entertainment. These are three reasons why Facebook has grown in popularity over its short lifespan. It provides a utility to those who participate that other platforms don't match. As a result, Facebook users are very free with the information that they share with other users—and that which they allow Facebook to share with advertisers. Most users will tell you that they don't want their personal information shared by Facebook. But at the same time, they will agree to the terms and conditions of the platform without giving a second thought to what those terms say can be done with their information. Sure, every once in a while there is a public uproar about what Facebook is doing or some change that it has made, but the public in general has proven that those things won't change their usage habits for long. It is that very behavior that makes the platform a great opportunity for advertisers.

The basics of the Facebook platform are simple to understand. Facebook provides a desktop and mobile version of its platform that can be accessed by its users via a single, persistent login across all devices. This single sign-on process across devices provides both a utility to users and a great data compilation tool for Facebook. The single-user ID that is created by the persistent cross-device sign-on process allows Facebook to see a user as an individual and not a series of related cookies. Each interaction that a user has with Facebook is tracked and associated with that individual without any guesswork or ambiguity. Facebook, in turn, provides access to this single view of the user through its advertising platform and gives you the ability to advertise to those individuals specifically, to identify properties for those individuals who are important to you, and then to look for others within the platform who have similar properties (look-alikes). It can also target users generically, based on that first-party volunteered data. The platform gives you a series of ways to deliver your advertising, including display or video ads that run in users' news feeds or down the right side of the page when viewed on the desktop. Facebook has added new platforms, like Instagram, over the last few years that have brought additional scale and new options for format and delivery. As we mentioned previously, the ad formats and targeting options are consistently expanding, and in the time it has taken for us to write and publish this book, there will likely be several additional advancements on this platform.

At the same time Facebook is increasing the ability to reach individuals on its own platform and in its own content delivery, the platform is also taking that information and externalizing it to reach people across the web. With the acquisition of Atlas, Facebook has begun to expand its ability to utilize its information to deliver ads that are running across other publisher websites. In 2014, Facebook took the first steps toward externalizing targeting capabilities when it began allowing advertisers to buy mobile ads on third-party sites using the same targeting features that were available within the Facebook platform. Then, in late 2014, the company announced the launch of a similar platform on the desktop side. Using Atlas as the primary delivery tool, Facebook is integrating the Atlas ad-serving technology with its own first-party user data and a consistent cross-platform ID for both targeting and reporting. As this toolset continues to grow, Facebook is pushing advertisers to think about its advertising in a Platform Marketer construct and to move to personalized messaging at an individual level. The company has stated publicly that it will continue to advance this effort to allow for more relevant advertising for both its users and its advertisers.

Google

Like Facebook, Google has built its platform to provide a social utility to users first and an advertising platform for marketers second. As we all know, Google began its journey by providing users with an information resource that they needed—and to which they very quickly became addicted in their daily lives. Over the past 15 years, Google has become not only a platform but also a verb. Within its search platform is a tool that lets users provide insight into their needs and wants, and Google then provides that information to advertisers to use as a means of targeting advertising. That is very easy to understand within search, but then Google added to that ability when it launched the Gmail email service in 2004, followed by the acquisitions of YouTube in 2006, the Double-Click platform in 2007, and the Invite Media demand-side platform in 2010. Through the integration of these platforms into a single marketing stack, the company has the ability to understand what people are interested in and use that information to deliver highly targeted and relevant ads to those users across search and display platforms.

Unlike Facebook, however, Google has not yet taken the leap to allow individual user ID targeting across those two delivery platforms. Within DoubleClick and the DoubleClick Bid Manager (the new name of the Invite Media DSP), Google provides the ability to target segments of users based on both first- and third-party user data that is shared between Google, its publishers, and in some forms, its advertisers. In 2013, Google launched a new targeting feature within the search platform called remarketing lists for search ads (RLSA), the first list-based search targeting feature in the market. Within all of these platforms, Google has given advertisers the ability to connect user interaction with websites to targeting of ads across the various areas of online advertising.

One of Google's key advantages in this space is that it provides a variety of services that tie users together across multiple platforms using a similar single sign-on process for all of its properties. Over the years, Google has made advances in providing personalized experiences for users and continues to develop new tools to serve better advertising and query responses to users of its services. This evolution continues as Google increases the penetration of additional tools like Google Maps and Google Now (a platform that is designed within the Android mobile operating system to answer users' questions, even before they ask them, by interpreting interests and needs from prior site interactions). Although Google has moved more slowly in the identifiable targeting space, the company has certainly moved just as fast as anyone else in integrating new capabilities for targeting within its various platforms and across their users. To this point, Google has relied primarily on cookie IDs for targeting by advertisers and utilized first-party Google ID layers for its own personalization. Today, it is making an effort to integrate CRM data into targeting for both search and display advertising. Google is also taking its targeting and measurement capabilities a level beyond other platforms by combining its advertising and site tracking reporting capabilities within Google Analytics to provide data on attributed cross-platform, cross-device, and offline conversion activity. As this platform continues to evolve and mature, Google is setting a precedent by helping advertisers understand more about the effectiveness of their advertising than any other platform.

Twitter

The newest of online advertising platforms, Twitter has made significant advancements over the past two years in both creative delivery as well as targeting platforms. Starting off as a utility for the dissemination of immediate response and new information for users, Twitter has advanced its niche in the online space through continued growth of targeting and reporting capabilities. When Twitter launched its partnership with Nielsen in 2013 to report on television viewer interactions on the platform, it opened the eyes of many advertisers to a new way of understanding the value of social media in recognizing the effects of offline advertising. After that announcement, Twitter also invested in its tailored audiences platform. Similar to the Facebook Custom Audience platform, tailored audiences allows advertisers to bring their first-party data to Twitter, in the form of email addresses, to identify and target advertising within the platform. This program has shown promise and will continue to grow as Twitter expands its reach and new ad delivery mechanisms.

The area in which Twitter has made the largest investment—and continues to show the most promise—is in engagement with users within the mobile environment. Twitter's first move in that space was to acquire MoPub in 2013. This set the stage for a new form of mobile ad delivery that would integrate social media targeting in the mobile ad delivery platform. As this integration continues to mature, we expect to see additional mobile targeting features as well as new forms of advertising outside of the Twitter platform, utilizing interest-based data from within the platform. With this focus specifically on mobile, Twitter has placed its bet on the continued migration of audiences away from desktop/laptop devices and onto mobile platforms.

Although Twitter is the smallest of the three top platforms, it has done the most to integrate its platform with areas of focus for traditional advertisers. This integration will continue to bring scale to the platform, which will fund growth of new ad delivery capabilities and, in the long run, position Twitter as an ongoing power player in the Platform Marketer space.

Scaling Platforms

Amazon

The Amazon Ad Platform and the Amazon Mobile Ad Network both show significant potential to scale in the addressable media space over the next several years. With tremendous amounts of data on customer shopping and buying habits, Amazon's platform can provide enormous value to retailers and consumer packaged goods (CPG) companies that are looking to capture customers at each stage of the purchase funnel. With the data that Amazon is already using, the platform will be able to provide indicators of purchase intent, look-alike purchase audiences, similar purchase audiences, as well as probabilistic sales targets. The limitation to this platform is that it is tied to purchase intent and entertainment behaviors. Amazon will not have access to life events, friend networks, or other indicators that Google, Facebook, and Twitter each have in abundance. That doesn't mean that the niche it serves isn't worthwhile. In fact, if Amazon were to open up more first-party data to advertisers and potentially build a partnership with another platform, it could add substantial value to any ad environment.

Walmart

Bringing a separate alternative view to the marketplace, Walmart has been more focused on using its ad platform and network to solve a different problem for advertisers: that of how their online ads affect offline behaviors. Sure, Walmart is allowing advertisers to utilize tons of online shopping data from its web properties for segmentation and targeting of ads, but the retail giant is also turning that information into ad justification by connecting it with offline purchase intent. Much the same way that Google is trying to solve this problem for retailers and service companies alike, Walmart's platform is trying to do more for CPG organizations to show that if you advertise on the network, your product will sell in the brick-and-mortar store. Advertisers using the Walmart platform can then also extrapolate that data to help justify purchases of additional online ads, based on who is being targeted, what purchases they have made in the past, and what they are likely to buy in the future. If you add couponing into this process, things get even more interesting as Walmart continues to expand the platform and use it as a means to show that customers still shop in both online and offline environments. This online/offline connection happens to be Walmart's only real advantage over Amazon for both advertisers and customers.

AOL

The AOL suite of ad platforms has continued to evolve over the past 15 years. We have seen AOL go from being one of the largest media companies on the web to being an afterthought in many circles of the online world. However, along that path, the evolution has continued and grown into something that is starting to look a lot like an integrated one-to-one addressable media opportunity across online and offline experiences. That may not sound like the AOL that you have come to know over the past few years, but it is certainly the AOL that you will want to know over the next few. Through the integration of its platforms, AOL is showing that individuals could be connected not only across digital devices but also on their televisions with the potential of Adap.tv. This makes sense for a company that was once part of Time Warner and one that has continued to push its media roots forward online. As the movement of TV programming online continues and the movement of cable providers to become more like set-top box digital delivery services (smart TVs, Google TV, Apple TV, Netflix, and so on) AOL begins to get the scale necessary to play at the forefront of the addressable platform space. The fact is that television advertising still sells, and no one else currently has the ability to sell television in a connected, consumer-targeted way linked to online advertising.

Apple

With all of the hype that always exists around Apple, it seems almost counterintuitive to list it as "a bit of a contender" in a space where it seems to have so much power. However, when you consider the significant reduction in market share of the iOS platform over the past few years, the question of whether Apple can scale becomes a concern. In a recent International Data Corporation report, data showed that while iOS devices were continuing to show sales growth, their market share versus Android devices was still declining (11.7 percent in second quarter 2014).[1] With that said, the Apple audience is still a relevant one, and Apple is doing its best to make the iAd platform one that will help the company generate revenue and drive its digital targeting business forward. The iAd platform has changed several times since its inception and, most recently, the big push has been to incorporate first-party CRM data to assist in targeting and to build advertising models. As this platform continues to evolve, it is easy to see the potential to connect iAds with Apple Pay and build something that can extend to other targeting features.

A LOOK AHEAD

As you probably realized when going through the details on each of the platforms, the race to the future of platform marketing is closer to the start than it is the finish. The major players we have discussed here will transform along the way, and new ones will enter the market from all directions. They will all evolve with the marketplace. There is the potential of regulation, the potential of consumer backlash on privacy, and the potential that a new delivery platform could come along and change the game even further (wearables anyone?). However, the one thing of which we can be sure is that customers will continue to react to increasingly relevant, timely, and useful advertising. When customers react, advertisers follow and platforms grow.

---

[1] www.idc.com/getdoc.jsp?containerId=prUS25037214.

Chapter 11 Measurement and Attribution

Special Contributor: Peter Vandre

For the Platform Marketer, effective measurement and attribution are more important than ever before. Measurement allows the organization to learn from the past and make better decisions in the future. It involves the development and ongoing management of KPIs and underlying methodologies that measure marketing effectiveness and provide insights for agile, ongoing execution. In spite of the proliferation of data, the advancement in computing power, and more sophisticated analytic methods, most companies are still struggling to effectively address the measurement problem. Companies are trying to take the same last-touch attribution shortcuts that, in some cases, were good enough before the digital channel and marketing explosion. Unfortunately, these simplified approaches are now leading to bad decisions and wasted spend. In this chapter, we'll explore the root causes of bad measurement and lay out the fundamental building blocks that are necessary to fix it.

MEASUREMENT CHALLENGES

The fragmentation of touchpoints, brought about in large part by the digital revolution, presents distinct challenges for the Platform Marketer. Consumers are exposed to a plethora of competing messages from offline and online media. And to complicate things further, they are reaching out to brands through an equally staggering number of channels. In fact, the days when an organization defined its brand and pushed it to consumers are gone. Consumers have just as much control over what your brand represents as you do. This is not to say that brand creation and mass media are no longer important. In fact, when you consider how much influence friends, online reviews, and social networks have on a buying decision, it has become even more important to manage what your brand represents. It is *how* an organization manages its brand that is changing.

Unfortunately, most marketers are still using the same measurement methods that were popular before the digital marketing explosion, a time when customer journeys were much more linear and simplistic. When consumers are engaging with relatively few media and channels, a last-touch or last-engagement marketing attribution approach gives directionally accurate results for direct media. Direct marketers have grown up using key codes for catalogs, dedicated 800 numbers for direct mail, and last-click/post-view windows for email. These methods inherently give more credit to last-touch marketing. As a result, they tend to lead marketers to overspend on bottom-of-the-marketing-funnel tactics at the expense of mid- to upper-funnel tactics. This problem is compounded by increases in marketing spend, a widening variety of media and tactics, and a growing array of choices for how and where to purchase. The outcome for large brands is typically millions of dollars in wasted marketing spend. Through attribution-sensitive analysis we have shown that, for many brands, a modest shift in attribution assumption can cut such waste by as much as 15 to 30 percent of the marketing budget.

The more effective approach to measurement, especially in digital and direct media, is to shape the attribution method to more closely resemble a consumer's actual journey with the brand. This requires not just looking at the last interaction that took place but the time sequence of interactions, or what we term the "event stream," leading up to a sale. The event stream

Shown
Display Ad
2/2/12 3:05 PM

Sent Email
2/2/12 5:05 PM
Opens Email
2/2/12 9:30 PM

Completes
Quote Request
Onsite
2/6/12 9:15 PM

DM
Delivered
2/1/12

Calls 800#
Requests Info
and Gives Email
2/2/12 3:06 PM

Clicks Branded
Paid Search Ad
2/6/12 9:00 PM

Consumer Event Table

User ID	Date Time	Event ID	Event Description
1234	2/1/12	DM437	DM Delivered
1234	2/2/12 3:05 PM	DI9076	Display Impression
1234	2/2/12 3:06 PM	CC068	Inbound Call Center
1234	2/2/12 5:05 PM	EM087	Sent Email
1234	2/2/12 9:30 PM	EM088	Opened Email
1234	2/2/12 9:30 PM	EM089	Clicked Email
1234	2/6/12 9:00 PM	PS674	Clicks Paid Search
1234	2/6/12 9:15 PM	Q8740	Completes Quote

Event Meta Data

Event ID	EM088
Creative	A2346 Insurance you can count on
Offer	O192365 $14/month for $25K coverage
Product	P978 Term life

FIGURE 11.1   Customer Event Stream for an Insurer

concept is relatively simple. Each interaction with the brand, outbound or inbound, is cataloged at an individual level, with a date-time stamp and associated metadata about that interaction. The output is a unique, individual-level timeline showing exactly how the consumer engaged the brand (see Figure 11.1). In the case that a company has multiple lines of business, it is a best practice to create a single event stream across interactions. For B-to-B, additional business dimensions are needed so that individual customer journeys can be aggregated and analyzed at a corporate level as well.

The event stream is created as an output of the identity management process described in Chapter 4. Event streams should be created for both anonymous and known individuals and, as much as possible, with an integrated event stream that ties back to interactions occurring across devices. With an event stream in place, we now have a robust data construct to allow us to ask and answer questions about how consumers are engaging across touchpoints. Equally important is the assignment of marketing credit on a fractional basis, not just a last-touch basis, to each marketing touchpoint. Advanced analytics, with predictive modeling or machine learning, are needed to do this assignment accurately. And testing is critical to validate the attribution process. However, our experience is that the Pareto Principle, or the 80/20 rule, applies to attribution. In this case, 80 percent of the work that goes into creating accurate attribution lies in the process of creating a robust event stream. Advanced analytics applied on bad data may produce results that are worse than last touch. Unfortunately, creating good event streams is very difficult. In the next section, we explain what the roadblocks are to getting to a better measurement system and what you need to do to move them.

ADDRESSING ROADBLOCKS

Roadblock 1: Organizational silos. Measurement roadblocks typically begin with the organization itself. Data silos tend to follow organizational silos. As an example, many financial services firms are organized by lines of business tied to product with separate measurement systems by business line. While there may be overarching organization-wide metrics reported, optimization occurs within product silos. Coordination across line-of-business (LOB) must occur to bridge data gaps across businesses and to more accurately reconstruct the customer event stream. For this work to happen, the development of a unified customer event stream and centralized measurement methodology must become an enterprise priority, and the overarching measurement framework must be an enterprise currency. Incentive structures need to be addressed so that marketers are rewarded for working across business groups.

Roadblock 2: Identity management. In addition to organizational challenges, companies also must be willing to invest in a robust identity management solution and continue to work on improving the quality of the output. This is a foundational building block of cross-channel measurement. Today, cookies are still the primary tracking mechanism for digital interactions but their effectiveness diminishes every day. Many mobile devices don't accept third-party cookies and many spyware/antivirus programs and some browsers block them by default. Additionally, cookies are tied to browsers, not devices or people, leading one person to have many different cookies from the same brands. Digital tracking based only on cookies leaves big holes in the identity graph and the subsequent event stream. Brands need to work with reputable partners to help fill in these gaps in a privacy-friendly way. Every organization also needs an identity management roadmap to prioritize and plan which improvements are introduced into the process and when.

Roadblock 3: Maintaining data quality. You can have the most robust identity management system available, but if you can't consistently collect, organize, and update the information about those events you cannot create a useable cross-channel data model. Our experience is that effective campaign data management is rare. Tags are often missing on creative or websites leading to data loss; campaign planners neglect to enter key campaign attributes or follow published campaign standards; and different groups and agencies working for the same brand do things differently. Additionally, data that may be correct when entered may need to be updated when more information is available. For example, original pricing terms for an online display placement may not match actual invoiced terms, once adjustments and discounts are applied. Incorrect information about a specific marketing tactic, especially pricing, will lead the marketer to make bad decisions if undetected and not corrected. Someone needs to be responsible for monitoring and enforcing data quality.

Roadblock 4: Walled gardens. Large publishers and audience platforms such as Google, AOL, Facebook, Twitter, and Amazon are creating marketing environments that are walled off from each other. Consumers traverse these environments, but these walled gardens don't always let the data flow with them. The result can be data gaps. For example, I may take a list of known prospects or customers and onboard them into the Facebook environment. Facebook, however, as of the writing of this book does not allow marketers to drop a pixel on ad creative shown to consumers in a way that allows us to target them within the Google ad network. Nor can we understand whether it is the same individual who is seeing ads in both networks. Effective identity management can help bridge some of these gaps, but it will not be perfect. Marketers and agencies have to be very strategic about which marketing solutions they choose (for example, DMP, DSP, and Ad servers; see Chapter 2 on Ad Tech Ecosystems) and on which networks they are certified for tracking purposes. Your media plan may help drive your decisions to utilize one platform over another. For example, if you spend a disproportionate amount with Facebook, you may want to consider using Atlas for ad serving, because it is owned by Facebook and has better tracking and measurement capabilities within that platform. Similarly, there are tracking and measurement advantages to using the Google DMP if you are spending a lot in Google's network. More on walled gardens can be found in Chapter 4 on Identity Management.

Roadblock 5: Offline to online data integration. Many attribution solutions are designed to work primarily with digital interactions and digital conversions. This may be fine if you are an e-commerce company, but it is a big problem if you are a multichannel retailer, a bank with branches, an insurance company, a hospitality company, or any business with spend in online and offline media and sales channels. To create event streams that span offline and online campaigns you need a deliberate data collection strategy to maximize these linkages. You also will likely need to leverage third-party data onboarders that can take offline identities and onboard them into digital identities in a privacy-conscious way. Vendors such as Merkle, Acxiom, and Epsilon provide these services. The end result of this process should be event streams that contain not only digital interactions but also offline interactions.

Roadblock 6: Ad fraud. In March 2014, the *Wall Street Journal* reported that "about 36 percent of web traffic is considered fake" and that about 28 percent of U.S. online ad spend is wasted due to fraud.[1] If this is true, it represents $50 billion in waste in the U.S. market alone—and this is a global phenomenon. Fraudsters are using bots and other methods to click on ads, browse websites, and even complete some basic online conversion activities like registration. The result is that basic attribution metrics, such as exposure rate, click-through rate, and incremental site traffic, are wrong. Finding and removing the fraud is hard, and the best defense against it is actually better measurement— specifically, optimizing programs based on actual online and offline sales instead of presale metrics. It is almost impossible for fraudsters to fake a sale. For this to work, we need to be better about tying online *and* offline sales into that event stream.

MEASUREMENT STRATEGY

The bad news is there is no product you can buy today that can completely eliminate the roadblocks for you. Effective measurement requires effective process and consistent standards, beginning with a solid measurement strategy and plan. Measurement strategy is a framework used to ensure an

---

[1] Suzanne Vranica, "A 'Crisis' in Online Ads: One-Third of Traffic Is Bogus," *Wall Street Journal* (March 23, 2014).

organization properly scopes and plans to implement a world-class measurement and attribution system. In our opinion, the best measurement strategies meet five key criteria.

First, a measurement strategy must have complete metrics. In other words, nothing is out of scope. A great example of this is the organization that spends a significant amount of money on broad media, such as TV. Often TV is used as a broad media designed to drive a softer metric like awareness or perception. It, therefore, is common to have a situation where direct and digital media are measured on an ROI basis but TV is not, because it was designed to drive a different outcome. Not having complete metrics makes the measurement framework break down, because how can we decide between spending more on TV or more on digital media without a full picture? Nothing should be left out of the framework.

Second, within a measurement strategy, metrics must be applied consistently. We regularly see organizations with a metric such as cost per acquisition (CPA), which they compare across programs. For example, digital display, paid search, and direct mail can all generate a CPA metric. Assume direct mail is measured using a test control design and therefore creating a true incremental CPA metric. But then assume search and display are calculated using direct attribution methods. It is likely that search and display will generate better CPA estimates than direct mail, simply because they are calculated using different methods. Calculating a metric like CPA in a consistent manner to represent the same thing across media and programs is essential to a measurement strategy.

Third, the metrics need to be applicable across all measurement levels. Marketing mix models are very effective at creating a single metric across all media, but this method can't estimate the same metric at a very granular level within media. Often, organizations use other metrics at a granular level like cost per click or cost per response. The challenge is that, at a quarterly or yearly planning level, metrics from the media mix are used to establish budgets and goals; each media owner cannot then calculate those same metrics day to day at the level of granularity by which the planning decisions were made. This is why it is essential that the metrics can be generated at all measurement levels.

Fourth, the metrics have to be applicable across all measurement dimensions. Dimensions in this context refer to common ways by which an organization would likely want to break out a metric. Geography and time are common dimensions. Organizations want to know what the cost per sale is by month or by state or by some other increment of place and time. Another common and powerful dimension is customer segment. What is the cost per sale by segment? It is important to plan early how metrics will be sliced by these dimensions. If we care about a metric like brand awareness, for example, we may need to increase sample size and ask specific questions to be able to report out brand awareness by segment.

The fifth and final critical element for a measurement strategy is to ensure the right method is used for each metric. There is no measurement method that is the best choice in every instance. Sometimes marketing mix models are ideal, sometimes random test designs, and other times market research is required. By ensuring the right tool is used for the job, organizations can often cut out some of the market research studies that are better handled in marketing mix models and then refocus that money to increase the sample size of market research studies in order to report out by segment or granular periods of time.

There should be two key outputs for measurement strategy: the metric playbook and the development and implementation road map. The metric playbook acts as a measurement manual of sorts. It includes an overall measurement framework, which is a visual representation of what metrics are important and how they relate to one another. This single framework needs to be understood and adopted by all groups within the organization. The metric playbook should also detail both the definition and calculation method for each metric. The second output is the development and implementation road map, which is a document that outlines what work is going to take place over time to build the required organizational support, the integrated measurement platform (data and data management platform), and analytics and reporting capabilities.[2]

YOUR DIGITAL DATA NERVOUS SYSTEM

Effectively estimating metrics is dependent on quality data capture and distribution. For digital, this is challenged by the myriad of ad tech partners that are required to execute a comprehensive digital marketing strategy. You are likely working with one or more DSPs, DMPs, email service providers, ad servers, search engines, search bidding platforms,

---

[2] David Williams, *Connected CRM: Implementing a Data-Driven, Customer-Centric Business Strategy* (Hoboken, NJ: John Wiley & Sons, 2014).

web analytics tools, content management systems, personalization engines, e-commerce platforms, or sales/lead management systems. Each of these systems is connected to consumer touchpoints and contains important information about what content, offers, messages, and so on were delivered to which consumers and when. These are the core ingredients that go into the development of the individual-level event stream—the data bedrock of effective measurement.

Today, most of these systems operate primarily through tagging and cookies. Tags/pixels are created by people and implemented in websites, creative assets, mobile applications, emails, and other places to enable data collection, proper content delivery, and browser-level tracking. Cookies allow us to maintain a persistent identity across touchpoints. The process of effectively configuring, contacting, and maintaining this data layer is often referred to as tag management. Effective tag and data management can create the digital data nervous system that will ensure that each marketing appendage is able to function in harmony with the rest of the marketing body.

There are tag management tools such as Tealium, Google Tag Manager, Ensighten, and BrightTag that are designed to help facilitate this process, but technology alone cannot be the answer. This nervous system should be actively managed by a centralized team that is responsible for not only placing and configuring tags but also creating and enforcing standards for campaign data. One reason these campaign standards are essential is that agencies and internal teams, by default, will not instrument their campaigns to enable measurement across the ecosystem, since these extra steps are often not necessary for measurement within their own silos. A centralized "data czar" or data group may be necessary to create and enforce these standards.

EFFECTIVE MEASUREMENT REQUIRES TESTING

Gone are the days when we could simply throw more analysts at measurement and expect better results. Creating and maintaining event streams requires technology. Attribution models are developed by statisticians or mathematicians, but algorithms are embedded in analytics platforms that automate scoring of new marketing data on at least a daily or weekly basis. The output should be expressed through comprehensive and centralized reporting that allows analysts to spend less time prepping data and doing custom analyses and more time sifting through results, finding insights, and making recommendations. The top attribution systems have gone a long way toward automating this process. However, often additional calibration of these outputs is needed to adjust for non-digital marketing touches, such as mass media, existing brand impact, competitive factors, seasonal impacts, and so forth. It is important that these calibration steps also be automated as much as possible.

Furthermore, the measurement discussion so far has been about how to understand the impact of marketing actions taken in the past. While these backward-looking approaches aid the ability to make better decisions going forward, they fall short of helping truly optimize budget planning. If a marketer has an additional million dollars to spend, should that be used to buy more spots on TV in Toronto, target deeper in direct mail lists, or spend more on targeted Facebook ads? The attribution models might suggest all of these as attractive choices, but truly making the best spend decisions requires drawing from historical attribution results and applying forward-looking analytics that can allow the marketer to run scenario optimization exercises and predict marketing impact. How many sales, quotes, prescriptions, subscriptions or new customers should the marketer expect?[3]

To support this capability, an end-user tool represents a best-in-class access capability allowing a user to engage with the platform and submit what-if scenarios. The tool draws from past results and predictive algorithms to provide scenarios ranked in order from best to worst performance. The output identifies optimal budget allocation across measurement levels and dimensions, including consumer segment. This provides a powerful differentiator supporting the Platform Marketer's ability to guide spend for next month, not just next year's budget.

TESTING

It is impossible to have a robust measurement system without a systemized approach to testing. For big brands testing is not a substitute for a solid attribution system, but rather an important complement. Testing allows you to validate key attribution assumptions and build confidence in the measurement system overall. Results of tests can serve as additional

---

[3] Williams, *Connected CRM*.

calibration points to the marketing system. For example, you might discover through testing that existing attribution models are underestimating the impact of a certain medium or missing an important interaction effect between media. Once understood, adjustments can be made to correct for missed effects.

In some cases, testing can help you fill in natural gaps in the attribution process. For example, as mentioned earlier in this chapter, Facebook does not allow marketers to place pixels on the ads shown to those targeted through their Facebook Custom Audiences onboarding process. We select an offline audience with personally identifiable information, onboard that audience into the Facebook platform, and then show them ads. We can track conversions that happen based on clicking on the ads, but Facebook does not allow us to cookie individuals as we show them ads. This leaves a gap in the event stream, as some individuals influenced by the ad search may go to a physical store or directly visit a website, instead of clicking through the ad. Here is where testing can help out. We create a holdout group that is not onboarded or targeted through the Facebook campaign. We then match online and offline sales based on name and address to those targeted (test) and those not targeted (holdout) and look at the incremental lift. This testing provides a level of measurement that is impossible to achieve without testing.

Testing can also help refine targeting and messaging within media. Programs that have a perpetual testing element evolve much faster than those that do not. This type of testing is informed through analysis of customer behavior, sentiment, and motivation, and married with marketing experience and best practices. We create an informed hypothesis for how we can improve performance, and then we test that hypothesis relative to our business-as-usual marketing approach. Test results should be cataloged and shared in a centralized way, yielding a strategic asset for the company over time. New marketers reviewing prior test results can benefit from years of prior learning and optimization.

Unfortunately testing is harder today than in the past. As we move to one-to-one personalized communications it is no longer about testing to discover the best overall message, creative, or offer for everyone but the best communication for the individual at that touchpoint. Testing variations can quickly explode and decision engines are needed that have integrated testing frameworks that can handle these variations (see Chapter 9, Channel Optimization). Analysts need to be trained in multivariate testing techniques and have an ability to prioritize testing efforts. As test results emerge, we need to catalog not only what the best messages are but to which audiences and under what circumstances. Through this process, we can learn a tremendous amount about our customers—honing our intuition and making us better marketers.

WHAT IS COMING?

Any measurement system should be designed with an eye toward the future. Although it is impossible to predict the future, we see some important trends that will impact measurement over the next couple of years. The first trend is the consolidation of attribution solutions within the major marketing clouds. In May 2014, Google announced that it was purchasing Adometry. The same month, AOL announced it was buying Convertro. What is the result? We expect to see attribution become much more integrated with the other components in the ad tech stack. Instead of requiring separate tags or ad server log file feeds, Adometry could benefit from collecting data directly from Google ad and analytics tags. Furthermore, attribution results could be pushed directly into the search bidding platforms and the demand side platform. Such changes could significantly reduce the effort required to implement the solution, increase data quality, and enhance the ability to take action on the results in digital media.

Facebook has not purchased an attribution platform but instead is bolstering the inherent tracking and measurement capabilities within its Atlas ad server. A shift from cookie- to people-level reporting and targeting is based on the platform's robust device graph. Today, these measurement capabilities are restricted to ads placed within the Facebook ad network. We expect Google to follow Facebook's lead and begin to allow for cross-device and persistent people tracking within its marketing cloud. By utilizing its robust identity graph, Google could greatly improve the quality of the consumer event stream. Google today allows marketers to onboard offline marketing touches, such as direct mail, and sales (e.g., call center) into the event stream.

The big question is: Will the big marketing cloud providers—Facebook, Google, Adobe, and AOL—at least partially remove their garden walls to allow for tracking across ad ecosystems? A Google or Facebook attribution solution is much less appealing if it can only measure marketing touches within each of their own walled gardens. If these solutions are opened up across platforms then we expect more of the heavy lifting around digital identity management and event stream creation to shift accordingly and independent attribution solutions to begin to disappear. If not, we expect independent attribution solutions to continue to thrive.

Chapter 12 Marketing Technology Stack

Special Contributor: Matthew Mobley

By now, marketing technology has progressed to a point where it has outpaced the ability of most marketing organizations to realize all the addressable marketing possibilities that lay before them. Technology in and of itself is not a limiter to the marketing organization. This is not to say that there are no limitations, but many of the technological barriers related to data volumes, access speeds, and connectivity to media and channels have been overcome. The challenges in technology lie in the ability of the marketing organization to rationalize all of the capabilities into a coherent solution that does not isolate data and insights in any channel or media. Every component in the technology stack, or platform, must work in concert with each of the others. They must have mechanisms to share data and insights, to deploy unified marketing messages, and to engage consumers in the context of previous experiences with the brand, regardless of the channel or media. This rationalization of the technology stack is where most organizations stumble.

There are many obstacles to achieving a rationalized technology stack, including factors relating to organization, expertise, rapid technology evolution, and overselling by platform companies. These obstacles are manifested because of humans, not technology. Another contributor to these issues is the lack of a universal marketing stack. You cannot procure a single platform from one company that will be able to meet all marketing needs. It takes a stable of technology providers to enable the marketing technology platform.

One quick look at your organizational chart will let you know if your CRM effort will be affected by the organization-related barriers around technology. If it shows a digital marketing team and a CRM or database team, you have a problem. This structure is very common in large and medium-sized organizations and stems from the fact that the skills required for digital marketing are not inherent in traditional database marketing personnel. But this organizational structure will result in two primary data and insights silos: one for offline CRM data, and one for online data. Each silo will make technology decisions in the context of its own marketing purview, and these technology choices will not readily align if and when they are brought together. Any technology decision must be made in the context of the entire marketing organization. Does the technology we are implementing enable data and insights to be activated in any channel and media? Does this technology share its data and insights with all other technology components in the technology stack? If the answer is no, you need to reconsider this component. The digital technology teams need to be focused on how they leverage the rich data contained in the offline world, and the traditional marketing teams need to understand the digital world.

Marketing organizations struggle to keep up with the expertise needed to understand all the technologies that are in play today and their hyper-evolution in the market. Typically, marketing technologists develop a deep understanding of specific components in the stack for specific channels and media, but fail to understand how these same components can drive other channels and media. This results in a technology landscape that is littered with point solutions that don't integrate with each other. It is further exacerbated by rapid changes in these technologies and new technology players entering the arena. As these technologists cope with their day jobs they are unable to maintain the level of exploration and learning needed to understand the dynamics of technology evolution.

The other expertise gap exists in the CIO organization. While these organizations have developed deep proficiency in core operational technologies, this expertise does not directly translate into the technology skills that are needed by the marketing organization. Marketing organizations also struggle with the lack of agility found in the traditional IT organizations. They have sacrificed some agility to risk mitigation and governance practices, which are important competencies to ensure success in their arena. They also have challenges similar to those of the marketing organization, in that the technology is evolving at a pace that exceeds the time it takes to understand the new technology sets. It will take a dedicated and focused effort by both organizations to keep pace. Unfortunately, this comes at a cost to the organization.

A RATIONALIZED TECHNOLOGY ARCHITECTURE

Key to creating a rationalized, integrated architecture is the development of a functional blueprint that depicts key areas of the marketing technology stack. This architecture will become the guidepost for key technology decisions and for socializing the vision in the enterprise. It defines the key components, each of which must be viewed with every other component as both a consumer and contributor of data and insights. It cannot include every function, but it should describe the broad platform.

The foundation of this platform relies on three core components: the marketing database, identity management, and the data management platform (Figure 12.1). These components make up the foundational marketing platform. Any success or failures in these components will be propagated and magnified in the other components. This is a result of the fact that these layers are responsible for storing, integrating, and managing the data—the lifeblood of this marketing platform.

MARKETING DATABASE

The foundation of the marketing technology stack is still the marketing database. What has changed in today's world are the types and volume of data contained within it. These changes force organizations to rethink how they build and implement the marketing database. The marketing database should no longer be viewed as a relational database with a set

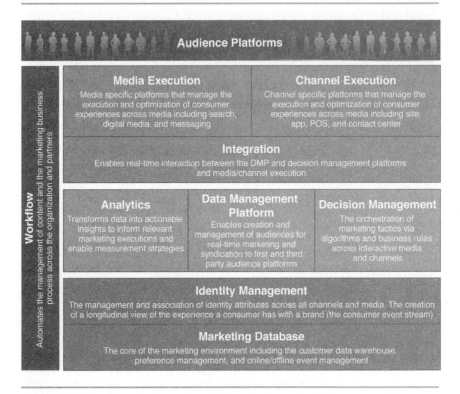

FIGURE 12.1 The Rationalized Technology Architecture with Highlighted Foundational Marketing Components

of applications to manage the marketing efforts. Traditional relational databases still have a significant role, but they only represent a component of the overall marketing data platform.

In the past, the marketing database was a warehouse built on a relational database structure. Marketing applications would be implemented on top of this database, or data marts were created to serve data to the applications. This model presents a significant challenge with data today. Marketing data assets have grown in volume and have introduced unstructured data to the mix. The volume issue alone can create high-cost barriers if it is implemented in the traditional structures. Also, in the past all data was typically associated with an identified person. Inherently, this would limit the overall size of the database. While these databases were still large, many times you would rationalize the data to a single representation of an individual. This would ultimately limit the data volume to a population equivalent to the size of the country, or countries, you were dealing with.

Today, you can have many more representations of an individual, because the marketing data platform will maintain unique representations of individuals that we may not be able to associate. These unique representations can be attributed to the many anonymous forms an individual may take in the digital world. The other big driver of data volume is the number of events—and their associated data—that must be considered in the marketing data platform. The digital channels have drastically increased the volume of this data. Thinking of the marketing data platform, you must consider the management of these data assets:

- Offline data: data associated to a terrestrial data identity, like name, address, and phone number.
- Online data: data associated to a device or digital identity, like a cookie.
- Structured data: data that can be easily classified and organized.
- Unstructured data: data that contains variable components that are not easily organized and queried by end users, such as consumer reviews.
- Known data: data associated to a terrestrial identity.
- Anonymous data: data associated to a device or digital identity.

In consideration of these new data requirements, we must look at the marketing data platform in two tiers, the first being the "data lake." This is the main destination for all data no matter what form it takes. This tier contains all data assets in a technology set and the mechanisms for assimilating and synthesizing those data assets into a consumable form to be used by different constituencies. The data lake is typically implemented with big data technologies. Big data platforms have made significant advancements and moved beyond novelty IT projects into a world where they are enterprise ready. There is still further progress to be made with these platforms, but many of the players in this space have created distributions that improve adoption in an organization.

The next tier in the marketing data platform layer is the relational database layer. This layer resembles the traditional models of the past, but its primary source of data is the data lake. It is typically implemented with traditional relational database management systems. Today, big data technologies cannot replace this layer, due to the fact that many marketing applications have not matured to a point where they can be easily implemented in line with big data technologies. But this is rapidly changing. Many of the marketing applications will have direct access to this layer of synthesized data coming from the data lake.

Data access and movement must be thoughtfully considered around the marketing data platform. Users will need access to the data lake to create other consumable data assets that can then be moved into the layer supporting the marketing applications. Each tier must be built with data democratization in mind. That is, the data must be free to move to any place by any user to fuel the marketing process. We must prevent any data management layer from creating a silo that will need to be broken down in the future.

DATA MANAGEMENT PLATFORM

The data management platform (DMP) is a close companion of the data marketing platform, but it fills a specific role in the stack. The role of this platform is to manage the data that will be activated in digital channels and media, as well as other interactive channels, such as the call center or a point-of-sale system. The DMP must contain a few core functions:

- Audience Management. The ability to view and segment marketing audiences based on characteristics and behaviors contained in the platform.
- Audience Syndications. The movement of targeted audience segments to marketing execution platforms.
- Business Intelligence. A simplified reporting and analysis layer to evaluate audiences and campaign performance.
- Data Interface. A rich integration layer that allows other applications to interact with the data contained in the DMP.

The DMP market can be broken into three core categories:

1. Execution DMP. The execution DMP directly supports a specific set of channels and media. It contains core DMP functions, but the syndication is limited to the specific channels and media. These DMPs typically lack a robust data interface, which limits their use across all channels and media. A good example of an execution DMP is one that is in direct support of display media. Many demand-side platforms will leverage this type of DMP.

2. Pure-Play DMP. The pure-play DMP, for the most part, represents the majority of the DMP market. It contains components of the execution DMP, but extends its value by including a rich data interface layer that enables the democratization of data across channels and media. Many pure-play DMPs also contain a data exchange capability that allows a marketer to extend existing audiences or acquire new audiences through a third-party provider.

3. Experience DMP. The experience DMP extends beyond the traditional role of a data management platform. In conjunction with functions contained in the execution and pure-play DMPs, these DMPs bring tightly integrated experience management functions to the table. These experience management functions can include optimization and personalization capabilities.

Obviously, choosing the right DMP is highly dependent on the requirements of the marketing organization, but considerable attention must be paid during the process. Every DMP is trying to extend further up the value chain. The reality is that many of them lack the most important thing. A DMP must enable data activation in any channel and media. In the absence of a DMP that can achieve this, an organization will end up with multiple platforms performing the same function for different channels and media. In the end, this has a high potential of creating data silos, ultimately fragmenting the marketing message.

IDENTITY MANAGEMENT

The identity management component is responsible for rationalizing the myriad of identity signals. It allows marketers to associate terrestrial, device, and digital identity attributes with a single individual. These associations allow marketers to connect disparate data sets into a single integrated view of the consumer's characteristics and behaviors across channels and media. This integrated view is then leveraged by other components in the stack to inform marketing strategies, measure marketing effectiveness, and guide the consumer experience. Identity management should create two primary data assets: the identity graph, or map, and the event stream.

The identity graph (Figure 12.2) enables marketers to find associations between events and identity signals. This graph must be accessible to all

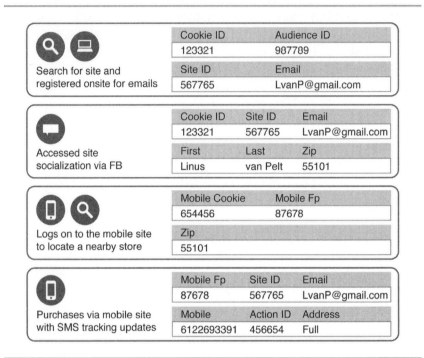

FIGURE 12.2 Rationalized Identity

other components. This access could be achieved by publishing the graphing to downstream components or by providing search access to the graph via a service.

As an example of how this can be applied, an anonymous consumer, while searching on the website, decides to sign up for a promotions newsletter. In the absence of the identity graph, we would only be able to leverage the data generated in the browsing session to determine what to say to this consumer. With the identity graph, we would be able to find out if this consumer is already a customer, and if so, understand the current relationship with the brand (e.g., what products he owns). This would then allow us to tailor the next message to the consumer. Instead of offering this consumer a product he already owns, we could offer accessories or services related to that product.

As a result of the identity graph, we are also able to construct a longitudinal view of the consumer's experiences with a brand. We can chronologically associate events across channels to a single individual

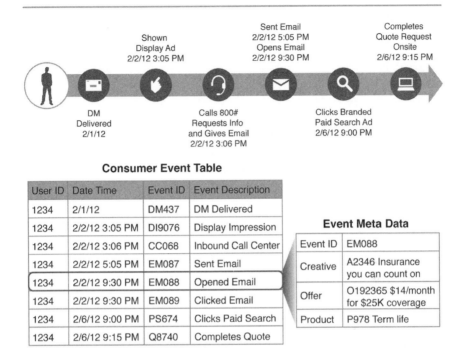

FIGURE 12.3   Longitudinal View of Experiences

(Figure 12.3). These events extend beyond just digital channels and media. They are inclusive of all events, both online and offline (e.g., direct mail, call center, branches, and stores). This ordered set of consumer events is called an event stream. With the event stream, we can develop a rich understanding of the consumer journey. This will allow us to understand where the consumer is in the buying process, how he prefers to interact with the brand, and what channels are most effective in influencing him. The event stream also becomes a key asset in the insights engine. It is used to inform customer strategy and measurement.

ANALYTICS PLATFORM

The analytics platform is not only a discrete component of the marketing technology stack. It is a function and consideration for every component of the stack. Analytics must be at the heart of every component. Every component is a potential data provider or operationalization platform for analytics. Too often in the past, analytics was an afterthought to the marketing platform. After the databases and applications were implemented, the analysts were given access to a platform that wasn't optimized for the work they were doing. The analytics platform contains three core layers: data, analysis, and operational.

The data layer tends to be one of the largest challenges for the analyst. Data tends to be spread across multiple components of the stack, thus forcing the analyst to spend an inordinate amount of time integrating data into a usable asset. Couple the data integration issues with the data volumes in today's digital world, and the problem becomes a significant barrier for the analyst. This is where architectures centered on the data lake concept can create advantage. Through the data lake, the analyst has the ability to gain access to an integrated view of the data and an environment that can process large data volumes. Leveraging big data technologies can empower the analyst to develop richer insights.

The analysis layer represents the set of tools and capabilities that enable the analyst to perform her work. These range from business intelligence applications to statistical workbenches with sophisticated modeling tools. Obviously, complete access to the data layer from these applications is critical, but it is equally important to have a platform that enables an analyst to ask questions. In the context of all the data related to the marketing organization, one should be able to perform rapid, iterative analysis and longer, in-depth studies of the data. As organizations implement these platforms and consider the big data issue, they are usually only able to accomplish the second, in-depth data studies. They typically have to deploy a secondary tier in the architecture to solve for the interactive analysis questions. While this is effective, it creates another separation of data that must be overcome. The platforms exist today to perform these dual roles without creating additional tiers. Organizations need to look beyond their traditional approaches and explore the more cost-effective, data-inclusive big data environments

The final part of the analytics platform is the operational layer. This part is not completely contained in the analytics platform, rather, it is a function of every component. An important consideration for the marketing technology stack is that analytics must be imbedded in every layer. Every component has a role in operationalizing analytics. Components are consuming insights through attributes deployed in their data models, or they are executing algorithms in real time and batch. Analytics must be in the forefront of our minds as we define and build each component. Any inability of a component to contribute to the operationalization of analytics becomes a major deficiency in that component's ability to contribute to the overall marketing program.

DECISION MANAGEMENT

Decision management is a core component for operationalizing insights derived in the analytics platform. The decision management component orchestrates the execution of algorithms and business rules across interactive channels and media. This is not the only component of the stack that performs this orchestration. Many times channel- and media-specific technologies will also contain some form of decision management capabilities. The challenge with these decision management capabilities is that they only support a specific part of the customer journey and may not be synchronized with other channels' or media's decision management capability. The best example of this is when consumers receive competing offers from the same company. A consumer receives both a 5 percent and a 15 percent discount offer for the same item. In the worst case scenario, this could happen on the same web page. This is because of fragmentation in the decision management function. There are two key considerations for the decision management component: centralization and interaction.

The role of the decision management component is not to encapsulate every rule and algorithm but instead to be a centralized decision engine to drive continuity across channels and media. Every channel and media can connect to the decision management component to receive an answer based on the rule set. Further rules and algorithms may be applied at the channel and media technology level, but these additional decisions will be working with a common base.

The decision management component doesn't just support digital channels and media. These may be the most common interactions, but this component supports any interactive channels and media. This would include things like the call center and the point of sale. Interactive channels and media can be defined as any channel or media that must react to data previously obtained about the consumer, typically housed in the data management platform, and data generated by the consumer at the point of interaction. The decision management component will have to combine this data, determine the outcome for the associated rules and algorithms, and return an answer in real time.

This may be best illustrated through an example. A consumer lands on a brand's web page. Through previous interactions with this consumer, we have specific knowledge of his interest in and relationship to the brand. When the consumer initially arrives at the site, a process is executed in real time to identify the consumer and determine the best message to display to that individual. The decision management component would determine this message. Additional decision management functions tied to the website may personalize the content that is displayed on the site. Later, this same consumer calls into the call center. Once again we are able to identify him. As the call is being routed to the appropriate service agent, the decision management component is queried, and it returns the same message that was used on the site. The call center servicing application then uses this message to construct a dynamic script for the service agent to use. The decision management component is key to driving continuity in marketing efforts.

MASTERING THE CONNECTIVE TISSUE

In the end, the success of the marketing technology stack rests not on the success of any individual component, but on how the components are connected together. If you think back to Figure 12.1 at the beginning of this chapter, one of the most important parts is what happens in the white spaces of that picture. An organization's technology landscape is littered with best-in-class point solutions. Each technology is chosen in a well-considered request for proposal (RFP) process that pits the functions of one provider against another. The biggest problem is that, while functions and capabilities are important, how well this technology integrates into the technology stack and enables all channel and media is equally as important. This thought is commonly overlooked in RFP processes—or is completely ignored because organizations are focused only on solving a single problem with a single channel or media. Every data attribute and every insight should have a shared definition when returned to a component for use. No one single component should create a silo in the stack.

As technology is considered to become part of the stack, a great way to think about that technology is as a hub for every other component (Figure 12.4).

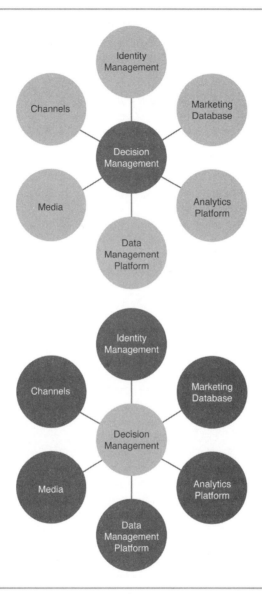

FIGURE 12.4   Each Component as a Hub

Each component will need to consume data and insights from every other component, channel platform, or media platform, and provide data and insights to the other components as well. Interconnectivity is as important as any other functional capability of the marketing technology stack. Any breakage will impact the effectiveness of your marketing efforts.

There are many other parts to the technology stack. There are workflow components such as campaign management software and content management systems. Each component should be evaluated and integrated into the stack in a way that prevents the creation of a data or process silo. The end goal of the integrated stack is to democratize data and insights for every channel, media, and user.

Chapter 13 Organizing for Success

Special Contributors: Leah van Zelm and Peter Kemp

Across industries, a common phenomenon is occurring. Customer expectations are increasing, budgets are shrinking, and technology is enabling an efficient, personalized customer experience. Mass digitization of media and channels provides the capabilities needed to deliver on customer expectations, but that's only one part of the equation. The other part of the equation is the operating model.

Historically, as businesses have evolved toward more customer-centric business practices, they've added functions and brought in expertise in the various required competencies, but in doing so, they've often created silos that hampered success and measurement. E-commerce organizations, for instance, were formulated as stand-alone units to test and incubate digital commerce, completely separated from other channels in terms of processes, tools, protocols, and policies. The approach makes sense in many ways—allocating budget to prove the concept; giving the team autonomy to optimize the experience, free of existing constraints; and minimizing interdependencies that may slow down success. Yes, these are good things.

The unintended consequence is that multiple channels often touch the same consumers, resulting in redundant activities that drive inefficiency and channel conflict. The customer experience becomes a by-product of the organization rather than a vision that drives the organization. Even today, call any airline and one of the first interactive voice recognition (IVR) options presented will likely be about whether you're calling in reference to an online or offline reservation. Because purchase channel is not a significant dimension of travel to a *consumer*, this artificial divide used to identify a reservation seems unnatural and awkward. It's a reflection of the lack of integration within the airline, rather than a purposefully designed experience.

Across industries, forward-thinking marketers must consider challenging the operating model, asking themselves some difficult questions, such as:

- How are customer-centric companies organizing for success?
- What shared services facilitate efficient operations?
- What are the new roles needed to drive mass customization and personalization?
- How do we maintain an agile and flexible environment?
- How do I get started amidst the unrelenting speed of change?

This chapter will address the experience-enabling operating model by highlighting the following important objectives:

- Start with the customer experience.
- Assign organizational authority and accountability for the customer experience.
- Embed platform marketing roles.
- Foster a customer-centric and agile culture.
- You are what you measure.
- Change management and transformation.

START WITH THE CUSTOMER EXPERIENCE

The typical process, as referenced in Figure 13.1, that results in the actual experience is this: Corporate goals are set; they are translated into

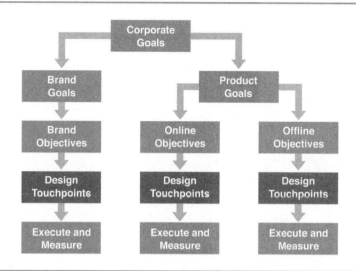

FIGURE 13.1   Customer Touchpoints Defined in Silos

product and brand objectives, with little to no regard for the customer strategy; they are further broken down to channel and media goals; at these different touchpoints, customer treatments are defined . . . in silos.

What's needed is an experience-enabling operating model designed around what's right for the consumer, *not* what's easy for the organization. Start with the experience to ensure that the rest of the organization can be designed accordingly. Figure 13.2 captures the concept.

1. Experience: perception based on the sum of interactions.
2. Interaction: activities in which the customer engages with the business to accomplish an objective. Interactions are where the experience is delivered through touchpoints.
3. Touchpoints: points in time where the customer engages with the business. Touchpoints comprise interactions.
4. People and process: internal assets that deliver business objectives and interactions.
5. Data and technology: underlying tools that enable people and process.

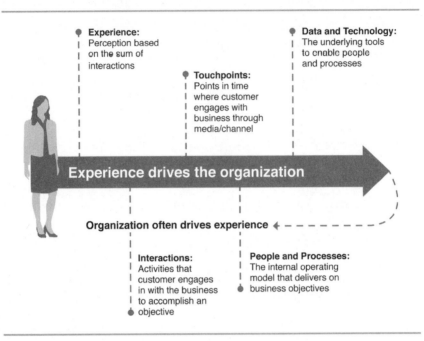

Experience:
Perception based on the sum of interactions

Touchpoints:
Points in time where customer engages with business through media/channel

Data and Technology:
The underlying tools to enable people and processes

Experience drives the organization

Organization often drives experience

Interactions:
Activities that customer engages in with the business to accomplish an objective

People and Processes:
The internal operating model that delivers on business objectives

FIGURE 13.2   Start with the Experience

The Platform Marketer must move from a touchpoint focus to a focus on the full experience, as shown in Figure 13.3, not only to drive efficiency in the organization, but also to drive financial value. Consumers rarely build relationships with businesses based on a single touchpoint. Relationships are built on the sum of interactions. Companies should start with an overarching customer strategy, which includes not only the prioritization of customers based on financial value and point optimization, but also a shared vision of the end-to-end brand experience desired, the interactions that will deliver the experience, and the touchpoint treatments comprising the interactions.

ASSIGN AUTHORITY AND ACCOUNTABILITY FOR THE EXPERIENCE

Organizational structure is about decisioning authority and accountability for outcomes. It's also about configuring teams to empower employees to best drive those outcomes. The two key dimensions that inform structure are degree of customer centricity and degree of media/channel integration.

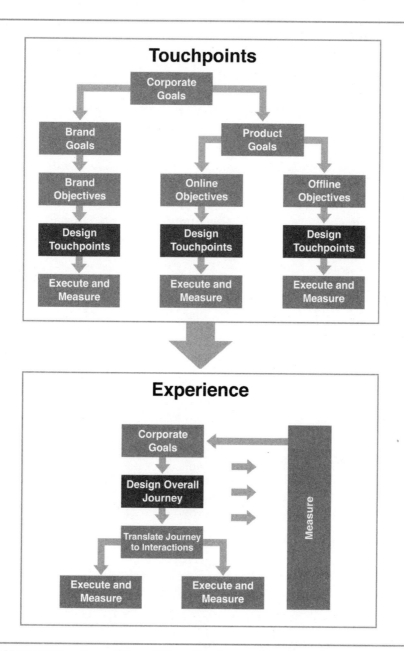

FIGURE 13.3   From Silos of Touchpoints to Integrated Journeys

Customer Centricity

The goal of a customer-centric organization is to maximize customer value and share of wallet through products and services that address customer needs. Such a model makes sense when the same consumer is exposed to more than one of the company's products or services, when customer knowledge is a competitive advantage, and when the customer experience is a differentiator. The more commoditized the product or service, the more critical it is to differentiate the experience. This is why financial services companies have been more advanced as an industry in the CRM community. A highly customer-centric organization has customer segment leaders with P&L and strategic responsibility.

In contrast, a product-centric organization maximizes value and market share by innovating on products and then finding customers to consume those products. Innovation, rather than the customer relationship, is the competitive advantage, and product P&L and share of market are key

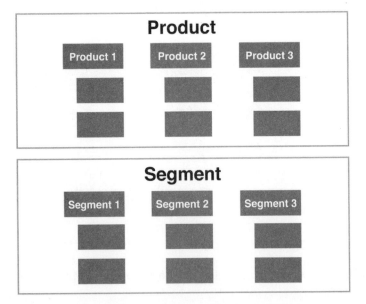

FIGURE 13.4   Basics of Organization Design

KPIs. A highly product-centric organization has product or product category leaders with P&L and strategic responsibility. Businesses in the consumer technology space, even when user centered in terms of design, tend to be product centric.

While there are many advantages to customer centricity, the reality is that there is a spectrum upon which organizations fall. Notably, the other end of the spectrum is product centricity, but it could be any type of division (e.g., geographic based) that is not customer based. Figure 13.4 depicts the concept.

MEDIA AND CHANNEL INTEGRATION

The next major dimension to consider is the degree of media and channel integration. The more integrated, the more efficient and effective an experience will be, which aligns with the bottom half of Figure 13.5.

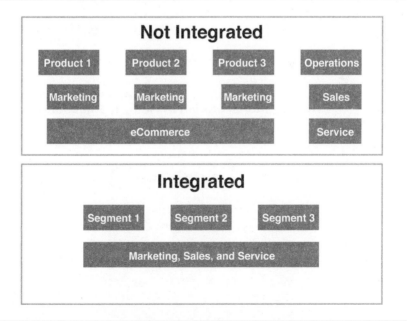

FIGURE 13.5 Integrating to Drive Efficiency and Effectiveness

AUTHORITY

Bringing these two dimensions together implies four possible organizational models, as shown in Figure 13.6.

The vast majority of businesses still rely on the matrix, and it is in this structure that platform marketing has been most successful thus far, as shown in Figure 13.7. The matrixed environment allows for product or

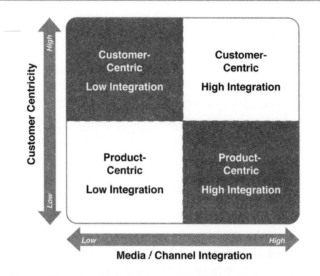

FIGURE 13.6 Organizational Models in Platform Marketing

FIGURE 13.7 Platform Marketing within a Matrixed Structure

customer owners to manage P&L, while a cross-product or cross-segment platform marketing team serves as an integration point among media and channels. The team is accountable to the P&L owners, coordinating budget and performance metrics; however, the platform marketing team is responsible for a portfolio-wide customer experience, delivering efficiently across touchpoints. With such a model, businesses not only achieve scale and efficiency and drive improved results, but there are opportunities for employees to build a career path, share knowledge, and learn new skills.

NEW ROLES

The platform marketing model goes beyond the new competencies involved in building relationships with customers on the digital audience platforms. It requires a fresh look at the organizational teams surrounding the effort. With the integration of media and channel and the opportunity of addressability at scale, new roles are necessary to fully exploit opportunities.

Chief Customer Officer

The most significant change is the emerging trend around the chief customer officer (CCO) role. There is a spectrum of authority among CCOs. Titles like chief experience officer, chief client officer, customer experience lead, even chief patient officer (in life sciences), are emerging. The CCO serves as the single point of control over experience across life cycle (acquisition, development, retention) and across functions (marketing, sales, service); the CCO also nurtures the customer-centric culture. It is still a new role, with an average tenure of two years, and more than half of the CCOs we've seen are internal hires from operations, marketing, sales, service, or general management.

To have a meaningful impact, accountability for the customer experience must be at a level that is senior enough to drive change for maximum impact, but some organizations are "testing into" the CCO concept. The continuum on control varies, and is summarized in Figure 13.8.

Low Span of Control Advisory	• Little direct control • Earn reputation and influence
Medium	• Dotted line authority • Owns budget but not P&L
High Span of Control Driving	• Has P&L and team • Direct control and decisioning

FIGURE 13.8   The CCO's Span of Control

PLATFORM MARKETING TEAMS

To exploit today's opportunities to deliver an omni-channel experience, new competencies (skills, knowledge, and experience) are needed. They are really an enhancement or a supplement to traditional marketing roles.

- **Consumer privacy and compliance:** While many organizations have for a long time had legal, regulatory, and compliance functions, today we are seeing these team members as a core part of the business. Rather than finding ways to inhibit business, today's privacy teams are evaluating risk alongside the business. With the fast-paced changes of the digital world, the team must also be quick to react, staying abreast of first-, second-, and third-party data availability and use, consumer expectations, legal and regulatory trends, and business risk tolerance. Responsibilities include:
  - ○ Set data transparency and control policy for the organization.
  - ○ Track rules and regulations.
  - ○ Interpret regulations.
  - ○ Disseminate information across the organization.
- **Audience management:** The audience management team is not unlike media teams of the past that figure out how to reach audiences via TV, radio, direct mail, and email, but today, the team has access to a much broader set of platforms. Responsibilities include:
  - ○ Define customer strategy and governance.
  - ○ Define audience.
  - ○ Conduct onboarding.
  - ○ Map and size audience.
  - ○ Develop strategy and select sites.

- **Identity management:** In the past, direct marketers have managed an integrated view of the customer, with the primary mechanism to develop that view being name and address. Today, identity management is much more sophisticated, as developing the virtual individual relies on matching cookies, IP addresses, email addresses, social handle, or other digital IDs. While this team remains highly data focused, the span of knowledge into *digital* data has extended greatly. Responsibilities include:
  - Identify and evaluate data.
  - Procure and intake data.
  - Support onboarding and list refresh.
  - Assess and audit tagging strategy.
  - Cleanse, match, and integrate data.
- **Platform utilization:** Reminiscent of call center systems specialists of the past, the platform utilization team focuses on what's possible in modern platforms (rather than just tracking call center functionality) from social platforms to wearables, the team is identifying the art of the possible. Responsibilities include:
  - Broker platform relationships.
  - Track and utilize platform functionality.
  - Support program implementation.
  - Identify and institutionalize best practices.
- **Measurement and attribution:** Measurement in the form of media mix modeling and probabilistic attribution gets enhanced by digital attribution concepts. Testing concepts still apply, but the tools available have changed, so knowledge of digital test design and data collection are now crucial. Responsibilities include:
  - Create measurement strategy and plan.
  - Manage marketing attribution solution.
  - Manage scenario planning and forecasting.
  - Draw insights and make recommendations on program, media, and customer optimization.
- **Experience design and creation:** This team is responsible for the omnichannel and media experience, including the creative, message, and treatment. Responsibilities include:
  - Understand insights.
  - Define experience for each key consumer journey (cross-channel, cross-media).

- ○ Develop test plan (program metrics) along with measurement team and optimization team.
- ○ Design program.
- ○ Develop and implement program.
- **Media and channel optimization:** The media and channel optimization team executes on marketing strategy, experience design, measurement insight, platform functionality, and audience availability to touch the audience. Responsibilities include:
- ○ Define personalization rules and models.
- ○ Develop media/channel plans and associated test plans.
- ○ Target audience with tactics, creative, offer, and message.
- ○ Reallocate budget based on performance, volume, and scale.
- **Marketing technology:** The name of this team is a bit deceptive, because while its members are responsible for technology, the convergence of business and technology is more pronounced than ever, so the team members must be more than the traditional technologists.

It's important to be aware of risks associated with the new roles. While the emergence of these different functions is providing organizational focus on these issues, it does create potential silos and/or redundancy. These new roles are valuable and necessary, but the ultimate solution is to restructure the organization to integrate these competencies into the new organization.

Another problem we have seen with the new roles is that unless they are integrated into a P&L and given real authority to make change happen they are often limited in their effectiveness. Top-down organizational support for these new functions, clear linkages to business value, and proper authority are critical for success.

FOSTER A CUSTOMER-CENTRIC AND AGILE CULTURE

Culture is the set of traditional and habitual ways of thinking and feeling within a society or group. Organizational culture should be nurtured and managed; untended it can be polarizing. It is the internal expression of the brand, and, arguably, the brand experience will reflect the internal culture. So, without the right culture, the customer experience can be disastrous.

Corporate culture is made up of beliefs, norms, symbols, artifacts, stories, legends, jokes, rituals, ceremonies, and celebrations that are particular to a business. In the era of the Platform Marketer, two cultural considerations are critical: customer centricity and agility.

Customer Centricity

Putting the customer front and center can be difficult when corporate objectives and KPIs aren't aligned with customer needs. Let's assume that the KPIs are aligned and focus on the culture needed to foster customer centricity.

Beliefs abound around the importance of the customer. Customers are talked about at all levels of the organization. Employees contemplate what's right for the customer, and decisions are made based on desired customer outcomes. This belief is reinforced by customer experience stories that inspire others. Artifacts, such as letters from customers or pictures of customers, are visual reminders of the culture. And customers may even be celebrated via appreciation days.

One of the most well-regarded companies in terms of a customer-centric culture is USAA, an insurance company that serves the military community. The CEO refers to himself as the chief culture officer; meetings begin with a reminder of the company's mission; new employees go through rigorous training to understand the customers' perspective; and employees are empowered to focus on customers' needs. Employees go through culture training where they "walk a mile" in the shoes of their customers by doing things like reviewing deployment letters, eating MREs (Meals Ready to Eat), walking around with 65-pound packs strapped to their backs, and reading letters from soldiers in the field.[1]

How does a customer-centric organization differ from others? Customer-centric organizations trust and empower employees to drive customer experience goals, and there is a proactive top-down appreciation for the customer.

AGILITY

The agile organization can further support customer centricity because the agile organization can react to needs faster and more efficiently than

---

[1] www.senndelaney.com/viewfromthetop_USAA_joerobles.html.

others. Such an organization is characterized by informed risk taking, measurement, reward for innovation and learning (not punishment), and the embracing of change.

The most well-known nimble companies are newer digital companies, and we find clients asking how to become more nimble when it's not already part of their DNA. Some suggestions include:

- Reward learning. When poor test results are shared, remind employees that the purpose of testing is learning, and it's better to get such findings on a small scale and then move on, rather than putting a new initiative into the market without testing. So celebrate those test results, both good and bad!
- Test everything. Test copy, link colors, targeting, usability, pricing, scripting, treatment, creative, platforms, devices, offers.
- Kill the HiPPOs (highest-paid person's opinions) by relying on data, not gut instinct. When a senior-level person (or anyone) has a recommendation, say, "Let's test it."

BUSINESS AND TECHNOLOGY ARE IN THIS TOGETHER

To succeed as an agile business, technology and marketing must work together more closely than ever. Historically, business has typically driven portfolio objectives by reacting to the market, being measured on product, customer, or brand goals. There's been little understanding of technology, which has been overshadowed by a strong drive for revenue. Technology has historically been about risk mitigating, process oriented with governance, and aligned with finance (focus on cost savings) or operations (back office).

The trend today is toward technology and the business sharing accountability—marketer as technologist and technologist as marketer.

As an example, Eduardo Conrado was CMO before taking on the role of SVP-Marketing and IT for Motorola Solutions. He says that his IT team is composed of one-half marketers with an affinity for technology and the other half are technologists with an affinity for marketing and sales. Motorola Solutions used the customer journey to define the tools needed to define roles in the organization. They built a marketing team with more digital and technical skills. IT creates a portfolio of systems, processes, and tools to enable the customer journey. The marketing staff works on technology enablement and a culture of collaboration supported by systems.[2]

YOU ARE WHAT YOU MEASURE

The final puzzle piece in the experience-enabling operating model is incenting the right behavior. This comes in two forms:

1. Compensation: Monetary means to recognize and motivate performance; includes salary, bonuses, and other monetary provisions.
2. Reward and recognition: Nonmonetary ways to motivate employees, such as special opportunities, employee awards, mentions, and attention in a visible manner.

Personal metrics must be linked to business objectives and must be done so at all levels. Figure 13.9 shows that this starts with having the right KPI framework in place to break corporate objectives (e.g., earnings before

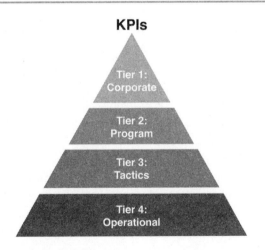

KPIs

Tier 1:
Corporate

Tier 2:
Program

Tier 3:
Tactics

Tier 4:
Operational

FIGURE 13.9   KPI Framework

[2] http://adage.com/article/cmo-strategy/eduardo-conrado-talks-motorola-s-move-marry-marketing/241354/; www.fiercecmo.com/story/internet-week-motorolas-conrado-says-cmo-cio-alignment-puts-customer-first/2013-05-21.

interest and taxes or EBIT) into program objectives (e.g., acquisition), tactical objectives (e.g., campaign), and finally, operational metrics (i.e., efficiency). Next, these metrics need to be clear to employees responsible for delivering on them, and there must be personal skin in the game.

The landscape hasn't changed, but the area of incentives is one that still has not been solved. Sure the tactics have, but from a corporate and programmatic perspective, businesses have to create value for consumers in order to create value for themselves.

It's easy to fall into the trap of the "folly of hoping for A while rewarding B," which I came across in the 1975 Steven Kerr classic titled as such.[3] Like other marketing eras, in the era of the Platform Marketer, we must be careful what we are incenting.

- Closing the sale or fulfilling customer needs?
- Average handle time or servicing the customer?
- Filling the sales funnel or conversion through the funnel?
- Within channel/media performance or cross-channel/media performance?

CHANGE MANAGEMENT AND TRANSFORMATION

All organizations are faced with the fact that they cannot be static; they need to evolve and grow over time. Change is constant, and we've just covered platform marketing related changes that the modern organization must consider.

Sometimes change is dramatic and sudden, like the emergence of a new technology or competitor; sometimes the need for change isn't realized until you see a gradual but inexorable decline in business results over time. The decline of companies in the "rust belt" happened over many years, and by the time they realized the world had changed, it was too late. Kodak realized the world was changing, but didn't appreciate just how fast digital media would replace film. On the other hand, companies like Nikon and Olympus faced the same potential threat, yet managed through it to be as viable today as they were in the film era.

Often the need to change requires an organization to find a new balance between the operational priorities of efficiency and effectiveness. Most companies find a middle ground between the two, but that balance may

---

[3] www.csus.edu/indiv/s/sablynskic/documents/rewardinga.pdf.

Efficiency Focus	Effectiveness Focus
• Highly integrated across functions • Focus on driving down "costs"—people, material, space, capital, time • Emphasis on process optimization • Willing to sacrifice customer service for efficiency	• Production/service excellence • Minimize risk failure when the cost of failure is enormous • High levels of customer service when it is a key differentiator and drives increased sales • Narrow functional focus to build expertise
Examples	**Examples**
• Amazon—pay less shipping if you wait for an out of stock item, so order can be shipped in one package • Manufacturing—Henry Ford only produced one version of the Model T and in one color • McDonald's, Walmart—limited choice, but relentless focus on low cost • Commodities—limited ability to value add, so must compete on price	• The U.S. military • Hospitals, especially emergency rooms—focus on patient safety • Financial services—regulatory compliance • Aircraft manufacturing—reliability, safety • Organizations creating a new capability • Start-ups—focus on getting product to market and later worry about margin

FIGURE 13.10   Efficiency versus Effectiveness Focus

need to shift toward one side or the other as the marketplace ebbs and flows over time. This rebalancing can affect an entire company or just a single operating unit. Figure 13.10 summarizes examples of this.

A good example of how this trade-off can ebb and flow occurred several years ago when consumer product companies responded to the emergence of new digital marketing capabilities by creating stand-alone functions responsible for "digital" or "social" outside the structure of the existing marketing organization. While this was successful in creating some level of expertise in those areas, the consequence was that marketing activities became much less efficient, as coordination across these new functions and traditional marketing was cumbersome. As digital expertise developed, it has become clear that digital is just another series of weapons in the marketing arsenal like radio, TV, consumer promotion, or public relations. As a result, most of those companies have folded the digital teams into the marketing organization. Likewise, digital ad agencies originally came into being because clients wanted agencies that were expert in digital versus traditional tactics. Today, even so-called traditional agencies have perfectly respectable digital credentials as well as traditional media expertise, and digital agencies are facing criticism for not being full service.

The need for change is fluid—you cannot just change the organization and be done. Change changes over time. If you are trying to change an organization (e.g. building digital capabilities), the initial change process may be the biggest part of the effort, but that is only part of the story. As the organization settles into the new structure and processes, it will need to continue to tweak the model and will have slightly different needs 6 or 12 or 18 months later. You need to build those future changes into your planning, so they cause as little disruption to your organization as possible.

SO HOW DO YOU MAKE IT HAPPEN?

Change must come from the top down, so that the vision is clear and all resources are aligned to balance efficiency and effectiveness through the change process. Leaders need to listen to their organizations from the bottom to the top, but change requires leadership, and once an informed decision has been made to change, it needs to be driven from the top. The types of organizational change can be divided into two broad categories.

Structural Change

If the change that needs to be made is structural and strategic in nature, the senior team can probably make that decision on its own. Examples of this would be the decision to sell off a noncore division or to acquire a company. In those cases, change is pretty straightforward. In fact, companies that do a lot of acquisitions, like GE or IBM, are known to have created what is essentially a how-to book for every acquisition that explains, in order, what needs to be done to bring a company into the organization. In these cases, even though the change may be major, its effect on the day-to-day workings of the existing organization is relatively modest.

Transformational Change

The other type of change is much more difficult. Transformational change is about changing the structure and processes of an existing organization. In this case, it is usually advisable for company leadership to get some outside, impartial perspective on the organization with regard to skills, resources, capabilities, attitudes, weaknesses, opportunities, and so on. Sometimes these types of changes can be accomplished with a small change in the organization—adding a position, moving people around, and the like. Often, however, those minor changes just serve as a Band-Aid, and a more substantial change effort is required.

The key to successful change management is to think of it as creation rather than change. You want to think about how to create the organization and processes that meet the needs of your business, regardless of what you have in place today. This can be hard and painful, but in the long run, it will create an organization that is aligned with the business and positioned for success—and that will benefit every stakeholder involved, from the CEO to shareholders to managers to clerks and line workers.

Key steps in the change process:

1. The "to-be" vision
   - An organization's structure and processes should be aligned to deliver against the organization's business objectives, so you need to have clear business strategies with which to align.
2. The "as-is" assessment
   - Conduct an honest assessment of the current organization and the processes within it. What's working? What isn't?
   - Capture feedback from personnel on how they think things could work better.

3. Gap analysis
   - Determine what is missing between the "to-be" vision and the "as-is" reality.
     - What is working that requires minimal change or that can be leveraged or expanded?
     - What is broken that needs to be fixed?
     - What is missing that needs to be built?
   - Conduct a best-practices assessment.
     - How does your organization and its processes compare to best practices of other companies in your industry or other companies trying to develop similar capabilities?
     - Disney has a business unlike most others, but much can be learned about customer service from it that can be applied to any business category.
4. Creation of a plan . . . and a team
   - Once the gap analysis has identified the problems to be solved, create a team with representatives from all stakeholders to develop a solution.
     - This steering committee will guide the entire process and be responsible for finalizing any decision and ensuring that all work streams are working together effectively.
     - Subteams will report into this steering committee on a regular basis.
     - This committee will also have access to senior leadership at the company, so if a problem arises, it can be elevated to the highest level possible.
   - If you use an outsider to help with this process, that stakeholder team should serve as its client in the process.
   - It is crucial that *every* function be represented in this process.
     - Get the perspective from all stakeholders, no matter how minor their involvement may seem.
     - Get ownership from each function, so no one can say, "No one asked my opinion."
5. Make it happen
   - Visible and vocal senior leadership.
     - Ensure resources are in place where needed.
     - Make it clear that no one can say they don't want to be part of the solution or opt out.

- Clear responsibilities
  - Make sure every work stream has a clear leader who is empowered to lead and to get the resources needed to be successful.
  - These leaders also need to be told this is an important part of their job, not just something they do in addition to their day job. They need to believe they won't be penalized if this effort reduces the time they have for some of their other responsibilities.
- Alignment of resources
  - This includes making sure other stakeholders or contributors realize they need to make time as necessary (i.e., be available for meetings).
  - If any costs are necessary to support the change—full-time employees, travel, consulting, technology—make sure that a budget is set up and clearly articulated to avoid surprises.
- Regular meetings
  - Some type of regular reporting needs to occur from subteams to the steering committee and from the steering committee to senior corporate leadership to make sure timetables are being met and to ensure there is consensus on the work being done.
- Training
  - Make sure there is some type of training or communication program in place to explain the changes to the organization. This could be meetings, brochures, or actual training sessions—the format doesn't matter as long as the communication occurs.
- Keeping it evergreen
  - Make sure some plan is put in place to review the organization and processes on a periodic basis—typically annually or semi-annually—to review what has been done and make any necessary mid-course corrections to make sure the new structure and processes continue to be effective.

SOME FINAL THOUGHTS ON MANAGING A SUCCESSFUL CHANGE PROCESS

- Start with a blank slate. You really want to start from ground zero to design the organization and processes that best meet the needs of the business and align with your business strategy. Try not to think of how to change the existing process/organization, but rather how to create a new one that is aligned with the company's needs. When implementing change, you need to break and rebuild the organization to generate real change rather than merely trying to modify what you already have.

- Honesty is the best policy. The change process will not work unless everyone is brutally honest. It is fine to promise anonymity as long as the comments are captured.

- Bigger and faster trumps slow and easy. While it is reasonable to attack change in a series of manageable chunks, the biggest mistake most companies make is to enact change too slowly. This is often done to avoid causing too much disruption or out of fear that people may get upset over too much change too fast. The fact is, this tends to just stretch out the pain and uncertainty that goes with any change process. You want the organization to deal with the change and then move on, not to worry about when the next phase of change will happen. When Kraft and General Foods were merged in the late 1980s, there were a total of 13 different sales organizations across the two companies. While the marketing organizations were merged within a couple of years, the sales organizations were gradually integrated over a period of more than 12 years—shrinking from 13 to 10 to 8 to 5 to 3 to 1, with a new reorganization occurring every two to four years (exact transition figures may have been different, but you get the idea). Because this was stretched out, the sales personnel spent much of their time talking about or worrying about the next reorg—when it would happen and what would happen to them and their colleagues (some people lost their jobs with each reorganization). Needless to say, this hindered the effectiveness of their sales organization. While the disruption from 13 to 1 would have been traumatic and challenging, think of how much more powerful that sales organization would have been if it had endured even 2 years of difficulty but then enjoyed 11 years of working in the new structure and focusing on selling.

SUMMARY

The technological changes facing the marketing community are significant and will continue to change the way marketing organizations need to be structured and the processes they use. While some of these changes can be managed gradually on a day-to-day basis, marketing and business leaders need to be prepared to look at change as a broader, more transformational process. It isn't easy, but if done correctly, it can help drive the organization to long-term success.

Start by aligning on the desired customer experience. From there, develop a future-state vision of the roles, skills, and knowledge you need to enable the experience. Define the team structure; empower employees to drive business results; align compensation, rewards, and recognition to drive the right behaviors; and foster a culture that mirrors the brand experience. Next, identify the gaps in what you have versus what you need and create a plan to close those gaps. Finally, act on your plan; make changes, both big and small, and most important, communicate! Ensure sponsorship for change, conduct training, set expectations, and gather feedback and input.

About the Authors

CRAIG DEMPSTER Craig has been a member of the Merkle executive team for nearly a decade. In his current role as executive vice president, he leads Merkle's Digital Agency Group, a business unit made up of 750 employees who deliver integrated performance media agency services across search, display, social, mobile, email, web development, user experience, and creative services.

In addition to his Digital Agency Group leadership duties, Craig has led Merkle's corporate development for the past four years. During this time Craig has steered the company's acquisitions of IMPAQT, a market leading search agency; Social Amp, a Facebook preferred developer that enables the use of open graph data in customer communications; Fifth Finger, a mobile first experience shop; New Control, a digital and direct agency; and RKG, a performance digital media agency.

From 2010 through 2014, Craig held Merkle's chief marketing officer position, driving corporate strategy for the business and spearheading the ground-up development of the agency's marketing communication, PR, and events organizations. As CMO, he led the evolution and rebranding of Merkle from a database marketing company to a digitally enabled customer relationship marketing (CRM) agency, driven by data, analytics, and technology—a concept now known as Connected CRM®.

Previously, Craig was corporate vice president of Merkle's Content Solutions Group, an organization that combined data and analytics to drive direct marketing acquisition services for Merkle's clients across industries.

Prior to joining Merkle, Craig had a long career at Metromail, and then Experian (which acquired Metromail in the late 1990s). Among his positions there were vice president of data licensing, director of market development, director of interactive marketing, and various sales management positions. Craig joined Merkle in 2006, after serving as senior vice president of sales and account management for Experian Marketing Services.

Craig is a frequent speaker and writer on the topic of CRM and digital media and has been published in numerous publications, including *Advertising Age*, AdExchanger, *DM News*, and *Ad Week*. Craig holds a political science degree from Hofstra University and resides in Ridgefield, Connecticut.

JOHN LEE As executive vice president and chief strategy officer, John is responsible for Merkle's growth strategy and the development of products and solutions across industries. John is also a strategic adviser to many Fortune 500 brands including DIRECTV, GEICO, Disney, AARP, and MetLife.

John has more than 18 years experience in management consulting, digital media, and CRM. Since joining Merkle in 2008, John has served in a number of leadership roles, including management of Merkle's Healthcare, Life Sciences, Wealth Management, Travel, Media, and Entertainment industry practices. In addition to his duties as CSO, John currently oversees Merkle's insurance practice.

Prior to joining Merkle, John played executive roles in marketing, distribution, and technology in Liberty Mutual's Personal Markets division. Previously, he was a member of CapGemini's CRM Strategy practice. John began his agency career in account management and strategic planning with Young and Rubicam, Rapp Collins, and iXL/Razorfish.

John is a frequent conference speaker and contributor to industry publications including AdExchanger, *DM News*, and *AdAge*. He is a graduate of Franklin and Marshall College and lives in Wellesley, Massachusetts.

About Merkle

A new breed of agency, Merkle (www.merkleinc.com) is a market leader in technology-enabled, data-driven performance marketing. For more than 25 years, Fortune 1000 companies and leading nonprofit organizations have partnered with Merkle to drive revenue and profit growth through relevant, personal, and timely customer interactions. Serving GEICO, DirecTV, Dell, Google, MetLife, Lowe's, AARP, and other market-leading brands, Merkle is purpose-built to leverage a full range of consulting, technology, analytical, and digital agency services to create programs that place the customer at the center of the business strategy.

Merkle delivers its solutions and capabilities through a Connected CRM approach, which provides a systematic framework for identifying, serving, and retaining customers based on their value, through orchestrated interactions that improve financial results, create competitive advantage, and drive shareholder value. The company has experienced a compound annual growth rate of more than 20 percent over the past 25 years, with 2014 revenues topping $382 million. With more than 2,600 employees, the privately held corporation is headquartered in Columbia, Maryland, with 14 additional offices in the United States and locations in London, Shanghai, and Nanjing.

Connected CRM and Platform Marketer are trademarks owned by Merkle Inc.

Index